Rejoice
AND Be Glad

TEACHINGS OF POPE FRANCIS

2013
Lumen Fidei
Evangelii Gaudium

2015
Laudato Si'

2016
Amoris Laetitia

2018
Gaudete et Exsultate

Rejoice
AND Be Glad

ON THE CALL TO HOLINESS
IN TODAY'S WORLD

APOSTOLIC EXHORTATION
GAUDETE ET EXSULTATE
OF THE HOLY FATHER
FRANCIS

Paulist Press
New York / Mahwah, NJ

Cover design by Lynn Else
Book design by Sharyn Banks

Library of Congress Control Number: 2018941301

ISBN 978-0-8091-5430-2 (paperback)

Published by Paulist Press
997 MacArthur Boulevard
Mahwah, New Jersey 07430

www.paulistpress.com

Printed and bound in the United States of America

CONTENTS

FOREWORD

The exhortation *Gaudete et Exsultate* was signed by Francis around the five-year mark of his pontificate and is the most important magisterial text of the Catholic Church on holiness since the "universal call to holiness" of Vatican II. *Gaudete et Exsultate* encourages the faithful to live in everyday holiness, in terms that express Francis's own Christian life, his Jesuit formation, and Ignatian spirituality: "Find God in all things."

Gaudete et Exsultate is not a systematic reflection, but a pastoral guide to holiness: ordinary, next-door holiness. But this pastoral text on ordinary holiness is also an extraordinary document because it reflects, and in a particularly transparent way, the personal spiritual experience of the pope, much more mystical than ascetic. The document is remarkably easy to read, and it does not need complicated analyses. At the same time, it is fascinating because it speaks of the spiritual path of the bishop of Rome, Jorge Mario Bergoglio, who did not hesitate to choose "sinner" as the best definition of himself. It is about the holiness of all the faithful, but it also offers a glimpse into the understanding of what it means to "be holy" for a pope whose predecessors in the last few decades have been proclaimed a saint or are likely to be proclaimed a saint.

The chapters of *Gaudete et Exsultate* offer the reader a spiritual accompaniment that is also remarkably honest in naming theological and ecclesiological problems of the Church of today. Gnosticism and Pelagianism are enemies of holiness because they undermine the health of the ecclesial experience. They are two subtle enemies because they tend to isolate holiness in elitist, intellectualist, or self-righteous forms of Christianity. This concern of Francis for the health of the spiritual experience in the Church is based on a view of holiness that is not individual but ecclesial: it is not a private, individual holiness, but is always in the midst of the people.

Balance in tension is a key concept for Francis's way of thinking. In *Gaudete et Exsultate*, the call to holiness is a call to find a way between extremes, also in spiritual life: "We are called to be contemplatives even in the midst of action" (par. 26). The chapter on the Beatitudes explores the balance between the mystical and the active dimension of Christianity; between the call to mysticism and fidelity to the prosaic taste of everyday life; between norms and discernment; between a personal, devotional relationship with the divine and social engagement. Most importantly, it is about the relationship between discernment and the law: discernment complements the inevitable shortcomings of the Church's normative dimension; Christians need discernment against the temptation of rigidity. Together with mercy, discernment is the other key word to understand Francis and his view of Christian life as a constant but joyful struggle.

Gaudete et Exsultate is exemplary of Francis's way of developing the theological and magisterial tradition of the Church and especially his rootedness in Vatican II. From the very title—*On the Call to Holiness in Today's World*—we see that Francis develops themes of the conciliar constitutions *Lumen Gentium:* On the Church (1964) and *Gaudium et Spes:* On the Church in the Modern World (1965). As is typical of Francis, this document does not use a proof text approach to the conciliar magisterium: it does not need to make a point about a particular hermeneutic of Vatican II. The most important sources of *Gaudete et Exsultate* are his first exhortation, *Evangelii Gaudium* (2013) and the document of the Congregation for the Doctrine of the Faith, *Placuit Deo* (2018). What is most interesting is that Francis continues in his re-sourcing of the papal teaching by quoting recent documents of bishops' conferences (all non-European in this document: New Zealand, West Africa, Canada, India, and two from the document of the Latin American episcopate, *Aparecida*), in a counterbalance to the mostly European nonmagisterial sources used (Hans Urs von Balthasar; Carlo Maria Martini, SJ; the Spanish philosopher Xavier Zubiri; St. Faustina Kowalska; St. John of the Cross; St. Thérèse of Lisieux; St. Teresa of Avila; St. Teresa of Calcutta; Charles de Foucauld).

Gaudete et Exsultate is a papal document that is not explicitly ecumenical like *Laudato Si'*, for example. But there is a broad appeal for all Christians and believers. It has a very visible emphasis on the idea of holiness as the result not of athletic asceticism, but of talk about a possible holiness *in this world*. It calls clearly for a life alternative to hedonism and consumerism, but without yielding to retreatism and apocalypticism. Ordinary holiness does not come from isolation—existential or spiritual. Francis is a mystical pope, and there is in him a particular mysticism not only of the relationship with the divine, but also a mysticism of human relations. In this sense, the mention of the theme of migrants and refugees in this document on holiness does not serve in this context as an argument of Catholic social doctrine, but pertains strictly to the need to see the relationship between the path to holiness and welcoming the stranger.

The Church is not presented here as an island of grace for the holy ones, opposed to the sinfulness of the world outside; the Church is not elite, and holiness is not a project that should be shielded from the web of our human relations. There is a holistic view of human life. For Francis, legalism and traditionalism are not a way to holiness. *Gaudete et Exsultate* can be seen as part of the vision of Francis for Church reform that ultimately cannot be satisfied with the reform of structures, but is always directed to promoting the universal call to holiness.

Massimo Faggioli
Villanova University

PREFACE

"The saints." This is one of the earliest designations of the Christian community, as we discover through a careful reading of the letters of Saint Paul in the New Testament. Most striking are Paul's frequent salutations: "To all God's beloved in Rome, who are called to be saints" (Rom 1:7); "To all the saints in Christ Jesus who are in Philippi" (Phil 1:1); "To the church of God that is in Corinth, to those who are sanctified in Christ Jesus, called to be saints" (1 Cor 1:2); "All the saints greet you" (2 Cor 13:12).

In this letter, Pope Francis offers an encouragement to modern-day saints and followers of Christ. *Gaudete et Exsultate* reads like an extended meditation on the true nature of the Christian vocation with attention to the particular challenges of living out the Gospel in today's world. It brings together several unrelenting themes that run through Francis's teaching, now five years into his pontificate. At the same time, it carries forward one of the fundamental insights of the Second Vatican Council—the universal call to holiness.

A much neglected chapter of Vatican II's Dogmatic Constitution on the Church, *Lumen Gentium*, points to the dignity and high calling of all the baptized faithful:

"The followers of Christ, called by God not for their achievements but in accordance with his plan and grace, and justified by the Lord Jesus, by their baptism in faith have been truly made children of God and sharers in the divine nature, and are therefore really made holy" (LG 40). It is fair to say that few Christians think of themselves or of their communities as "holy," as drawing their life from the gift of God's own life. Pope Francis's "modest goal" is to "repropose" this teaching for our times.

Readers from all walks of life will find here much wisdom and encouragement for their daily journey in the footsteps of Christ. Holiness, Francis tells us, is not an affair for a spiritual elite or a coterie of extraordinary heroes. While the Church holds up the example of extraordinary models in the liturgical calendar to inspire us all, for the most part holiness is lived out by the millions of unnamed men and women who give of themselves in ordinary quotidian tasks, in their care-full attention to the small stuff, the accumulation of "small gestures" and "little details" as they care for children, spouses, elderly parents, coworkers, neighbors, communities.

Francis grounds his teaching not in highfalutin theological categories, but in the teaching of Jesus. The crux of his reflection is an extended meditation on the Beatitudes, Jesus's teaching in the sermon on the mount (Matt 5:3–11). The Beatitudes are a challenging message concerning the nature of true happiness—not the shallow pleasures of consumerism in a materialistic world, nor the self-satisfaction and complacency of deceptive and individualistic self-help spiritualities. Christian joy, he tells us, is not a flight from the inevitable sufferings, humiliations, misunderstandings, and even persecutions that come with authentic living. True joy is not the product of our efforts or achievements, but a sheer gift from God, "a happiness that the world will not be able to take from us" (John 16:22).

Pope Francis has placed the spiritual gift of joy at the heart of his teaching, beginning with his apostolic exhortation The Joy of the Gospel, *Evangelii Gaudium* (2013), in his encyclical On Care for Our Common Home, *Laudato Si'* (2015)—which begins and ends with a note of joyful praise for the marvels of creation, and continues in the postsynodal apostolic exhortation The Joy of Love, *Amoris Laetitia* (2016). He knows, as one theologian has thoughtfully observed, that it is simply impossible to be sad in Jesus's presence. Joy, after charity, is among the first and most incontrovertible fruits of the spirit at work in us (Gal 5:22–23). True joy and a good sense of humor are marks of genuine holiness, signs of the consolation that St. Ignatius of Loyola invites us to seek and attend to in the practice of Christian discernment.

The true measure of holiness, Francis rightfully insists, is not a self-referential preoccupation with a state of interiority, but is realized in what we *do*, in how we live each day. The way we choose to live with and serve others is a reflection of what is in our heart. Jesus's teaching concerning the judgment of God is presented as the "great criterion" which allows us to distinguish between true and false notions of holiness. Feeding the hungry, giving drink to those who thirst, welcoming the stranger, clothing the naked, caring for the sick, visiting those in prison—these are signs of the beatitude of mercy in action (Matt 25:35–36). True holiness, he tells us, is not a flight from the world with all its sufferings and confusion.

Francis warns against false notions of holiness, which he aligns with the ancient heresies of Gnosticism and Pelagianism. Both are forms of spiritual elitism, know-it-all-ism, holier-than-thou-ism. He exposes the hollowness of distorted forms of Christian living that masquerade as holiness today—including the virtual communities competing for attention on the World Wide Web and in the blogosphere. The rigidly doctrinaire, those obsessed with liturgical and spiritual exercises, are often coldhearted and blind to the true needs of those around them—the poor, the refugee, the neighbor in crisis. At the same time, the social activist who neglects the need for silent time in the presence of Christ or for the reading of the Word risks being carried away in an idealism without deep roots. True holiness is reflected in a healthy balance between personal encounter with Christ and an outpouring of self-giving love in service to others, in lives that reproduce the pattern of paschal love.

Modern-day saints live in a world where the signposts of faith are increasingly absent or obscure. In such a context, Christian communities face the formidable challenge of forming men and women capable of discernment—of distinguishing the fruits of God's Spirit from the many options vying for our attention. This letter is an excellent resource for Christian faith formation and should be required reading for thoughtful

Catholic individuals and faith communities. It invites us to rediscover the dignity of our participation in that great cloud of witnesses, the Communion of Saints.

> *Therefore, since we are surrounded by so great a cloud of witnesses, let us also lay aside every weight and the sin that clings so closely, and let us run with perseverance the race that is set before us, looking to Jesus the pioneer and perfecter of our faith, who for the sake of the joy that was set before him endured the cross, disregarding its shame, and has taken his seat at the right hand of the throne of God* (Heb 12:1–2).

Pope Francis bids us to "not grow weary or lose heart" as we press forward in faith's journey.

Catherine E. Clifford
Saint Paul University, Ottawa

1. "REJOICE AND BE GLAD" (*Mt* 5:12), Jesus tells those persecuted or humiliated for his sake. The Lord asks everything of us, and in return he offers us true life, the happiness for which we were created. He wants us to be saints and not to settle for a bland and mediocre existence. The call to holiness is present in various ways from the very first pages of the Bible. We see it expressed in the Lord's words to Abraham: "Walk before me, and be blameless" (*Gen* 17:1).

2. What follows is not meant to be a treatise on holiness, containing definitions and distinctions helpful for understanding this important subject, or a discussion of the various means of sanctification. My modest goal is to repropose the call to holiness in a practical way for our own time, with all its risks, challenges and opportunities. For the Lord has chosen each one of us "to be holy and blameless before him in love" (*Eph* 1:4).

CHAPTER ONE

THE CALL TO HOLINESS

THE SAINTS WHO ENCOURAGE AND ACCOMPANY US

3. The Letter to the Hebrews presents a number of testimonies that encourage us to "run with perseverance the race that is set before us" (12:1). It speaks of Abraham, Sarah, Moses, Gideon and others (cf. 11:1-12:3). Above all, it invites us to realize that "a great cloud of witnesses" (12:1) impels us to advance constantly towards the goal. These witnesses may include our own mothers, grandmothers or other loved ones (cf. *2 Tim* 1:5). Their lives may not always have been perfect, yet even amid their faults and failings they kept moving forward and proved pleasing to the Lord.

4. The saints now in God's presence preserve their bonds of love and communion with us. The Book of Revelation attests to this when it speaks of the intercession of the martyrs: "I saw under the altar the souls of those who had been slain for the word of God and for the witness they had borne; they cried out with a loud voice, 'O sovereign Lord, holy and true, how long will it be before you judge?'" (6:9-10). Each of us can say: "Surrounded, led and guided by the friends of God... I do not have to carry alone what, in truth, I could never carry alone. All the saints of God are there to protect me, to sustain me and to carry me".[1]

5. The processes of beatification and canonization recognize the signs of heroic virtue, the sacrifice of one's life in martyrdom, and certain cases where a life is constantly offered for others, even until death. This shows an exemplary imitation of Christ, one worthy of the admiration of the faithful.[2] We can think, for example, of Blessed Maria Gabriella Sagheddu, who offered her life for the unity of Christians.

THE SAINTS "NEXT DOOR"

6. Nor need we think only of those already beatified and canonized. The Holy Spirit bestows holiness in abundance among God's holy and faithful people, for "it has pleased God to make men and women holy and to save them, not as individuals without any bond between them, but rather as a people who might acknowledge him in truth and serve him in holiness".[3] In salvation history, the Lord saved one people. We are

---

[1] Benedict XVI, *Homily for the Solemn Inauguration of the Petrine Ministry* (24 April 2005): AAS 97 (2005), 708.

[2] This always presumes a reputation of holiness and the exercise, at least to an ordinary degree, of the Christian virtues: cf. Motu Proprio *Maiorem Hac Dilectionem* (11 July 2017), Art. 2c: *L'Osservatore Romano*, 12 July 2017, p. 8.

[3] Second Vatican Ecumenical Council, Dogmatic Constitution on the Church *Lumen Gentium*, 9.

never completely ourselves unless we belong to a people. That is why no one is saved alone, as an isolated individual. Rather, God draws us to himself, taking into account the complex fabric of interpersonal relationships present in a human community. God wanted to enter into the life and history of a people.

7. I like to contemplate the holiness present in the patience of God's people: in those parents who raise their children with immense love, in those men and women who work hard to support their families, in the sick, in elderly religious who never lose their smile. In their daily perseverance I see the holiness of the Church militant. Very often it is a holiness found in our next-door neighbors, those who, living in our midst, reflect God's presence. We might call them "the middle class of holiness".[4]

8. Let us be spurred on by the signs of holiness that the Lord shows us through the humblest members of that people which "shares also in Christ's prophetic office, spreading abroad a living witness to him, especially by means of a life of faith and charity".[5] We should consider the fact that, as Saint Teresa Benedicta of the Cross suggests, real history is made by so many of them. As she writes: "The greatest figures of prophecy and sanctity step forth out of the darkest night. But for the most part, the formative stream of the mystical life

---

[4] Cf. Joseph Malegue, *Pierres noires. Les classes moyennes du Salut*, Paris, 1958.

[5] Second Vatican Ecumenical Council, Dogmatic Constitution on the Church *Lumen Gentium*, 12.

remains invisible. Certainly the most decisive turning points in world history are substantially co-determined by souls whom no history book ever mentions. And we will only find out about those souls to whom we owe the decisive turning points in our personal lives on the day when all that is hidden is revealed".[6]

9. Holiness is the most attractive face of the Church. But even outside the Catholic Church and in very different contexts, the Holy Spirit raises up "signs of his presence which help Christ's followers".[7] Saint John Paul II reminded us that "the witness to Christ borne even to the shedding of blood has become a common inheritance of Catholics, Orthodox, Anglicans and Protestants".[8] In the moving ecumenical commemoration held in the Colosseum during the Great Jubilee of the Year 2000, he stated that the martyrs are "a heritage which speaks more powerfully than all the causes of division".[9]

THE LORD CALLS

10. All this is important. Yet with this Exhortation I would like to insist primarily on the call to holiness

[6] *Verborgenes Leben und Epiphanie*: GW XI, 145.
[7] John Paul II, Encyclical Letter *Novo Millennio Ineunte* (6 January 2001), 56: AAS 93 (2001), 307.
[8] Encyclical Letter *Tertio Millennio Adveniente* (10 November 1994), 37: AAS 87 (1995), 29.
[9] Homily for the Ecumenical Commemoration of Witnesses to the Faith in the Twentieth Century (7 May 2000), 5: AAS 92 (2000), 680-681.

that the Lord addresses to each of us, the call that he also addresses, personally, to you: "Be holy, for I am holy" (*Lev* 11:44; cf. *1 Pet* 1:16). The Second Vatican Council stated this clearly: "Strengthened by so many and such great means of salvation, all the faithful, whatever their condition or state, are called by the Lord – each in his or her own way – to that perfect holiness by which the Father himself is perfect".[10]

11. "Each in his or her own way" the Council says. We should not grow discouraged before examples of holiness that appear unattainable. There are some testimonies that may prove helpful and inspiring, but that we are not meant to copy, for that could even lead us astray from the one specific path that the Lord has in mind for us. The important thing is that each believer discern his or her own path, that they bring out the very best of themselves, the most personal gifts that God has placed in their hearts (cf. *1 Cor* 12:7), rather than hopelessly trying to imitate something not meant for them. We are all called to be witnesses, but there are many actual ways of bearing witness.[11] Indeed, when the great mystic, Saint John of the Cross, wrote his *Spiritual Canticle*, he preferred to avoid hard and fast rules for all. He explained that his verses were composed so that everyone could benefit from them

---

[10] Dogmatic Constitution on the Church *Lumen Gentium*, 11.

[11] Cf. Hans Urs von Balthasar, "Theology and Holiness", in *Communio* 14/4 (1987), 345.

"in his or her own way".[12] For God's life is communicated "to some in one way and to others in another".[13]

12. Within these various forms, I would stress too that
the "genius of woman" is seen in feminine styles of holiness, which are an essential means of reflecting God's
holiness in this world. Indeed, in times when women
tended to be most ignored or overlooked, the Holy
Spirit raised up saints whose attractiveness produced
new spiritual vigor and important reforms in the
Church. We can mention Saint Hildegard of Bingen,
Saint Bridget, Saint Catherine of Siena, Saint Teresa of
Avila and Saint Thérèse of Lisieux. But I think too of
all those unknown or forgotten women who, each in
her own way, sustained and transformed families and
communities by the power of their witness.

13. This should excite and encourage us to give our
all and to embrace that unique plan that God willed
for each of us from eternity: "Before I formed you in
the womb I knew you, and before you were born I
consecrated you" (*Jer* 1:5).

For you too

14. To be holy does not require being a bishop, a
priest or a religious. We are frequently tempted to
think that holiness is only for those who can withdraw
from ordinary affairs to spend much time in prayer.

[12] *Spiritual Canticle*, Red. B, Prologue, 2.
[13] Cf. *ibid.*, 14-15, 2.

That is not the case. We are all called to be holy by living our lives with love and by bearing witness in everything we do, wherever we find ourselves. Are you called to the consecrated life? Be holy by living out your commitment with joy. Are you married? Be holy by loving and caring for your husband or wife, as Christ does for the Church. Do you work for a living? Be holy by laboring with integrity and skill in the service of your brothers and sisters. Are you a parent or grandparent? Be holy by patiently teaching the little ones how to follow Jesus. Are you in a position of authority? Be holy by working for the common good and renouncing personal gain.[14]

15. Let the grace of your baptism bear fruit in a path of holiness. Let everything be open to God; turn to him in every situation. Do not be dismayed, for you can do this in the power of the Holy Spirit, and holiness, in the end, is the fruit of the Holy Spirit in your life (cf. *Gal* 5:22-23). When you feel the temptation to dwell on your own weakness, raise your eyes to Christ crucified and say: "Lord, I am a poor sinner, but you can work the miracle of making me a little bit better". In the Church, holy yet made up of sinners, you will find everything you need to grow towards holiness. The Lord has bestowed on the Church the gifts of scripture, the sacraments, holy places, living communities, the witness of the saints

---

[14] Cf. *Catechesis*, General Audience of 19 November 2014: *Insegnamenti* II/2 (2014), 555.

and a multifaceted beauty that proceeds from God's love, "like a bride bedecked with jewels" (*Is* 61:10).

16 This holiness to which the Lord calls you will grow through small gestures. Here is an example: a woman goes shopping, she meets a neighbor and they begin to speak, and the gossip starts. But she says in her heart: "No, I will not speak badly of anyone". This is a step forward in holiness. Later, at home, one of her children wants to talk to her about his hopes and dreams, and even though she is tired, she sits down and listens with patience and love. That is another sacrifice that brings holiness. Later she experiences some anxiety, but recalling the love of the Virgin Mary, she takes her rosary and prays with faith. Yet another path of holiness. Later still, she goes out onto the street, encounters a poor person and stops to say a kind word to him. One more step.

17. At times, life presents great challenges. Through them, the Lord calls us anew to a conversion that can make his grace more evident in our lives, "in order that we may share his holiness" (*Heb* 12:10). At other times, we need only find a more perfect way of doing what we are already doing: "There are inspirations that tend solely to perfect in an extraordinary way the ordinary things we do in life".[15] When Cardinal François-Xavier Nguyên van Thuân was imprisoned, he refused to waste time waiting for the day he would be set free. Instead, he chose "to live the present

[15] Francis de Sales, *Treatise on the Love of God*, VIII, 11.

moment, filling it to the brim with love". He decided: "I will seize the occasions that present themselves every day; I will accomplish ordinary actions in an extraordinary way".[16]

18. In this way, led by God's grace, we shape by many small gestures the holiness God has willed for us, not as men and women sufficient unto ourselves but rather "as good stewards of the manifold grace of God" (*1 Pet* 4:10). The New Zealand bishops rightly teach us that we are capable of loving with the Lord's unconditional love, because the risen Lord shares his powerful life with our fragile lives: "His love set no limits and, once given, was never taken back. It was unconditional and remained faithful. To love like that is not easy because we are often so weak. But just to try to love as Christ loved us shows that Christ shares his own risen life with us. In this way, our lives demonstrate his power at work – even in the midst of human weakness".[17]

YOUR MISSION IN CHRIST

19. A Christian cannot think of his or her mission on earth without seeing it as a path of holiness, for "this is the will of God, your sanctification" (*1 Thess* 4:3). Each saint is a mission, planned by the Father to reflect

[16] *Five Loaves and Two Fish*, Pauline Books and Media, 2003, pp. 9, 13.
[17] New Zealand Catholic Bishops' Conference, *Healing Love*, 1 January 1988.

and embody, at a specific moment in history, a certain aspect of the Gospel.

20. That mission has its fullest meaning in Christ, and can only be understood through him. At its core, holiness is experiencing, in union with Christ, the mysteries of his life. It consists in uniting ourselves to the Lord's death and resurrection in a unique and personal way, constantly dying and rising anew with him. But it can also entail reproducing in our own lives various aspects of Jesus' earthly life: his hidden life, his life in community, his closeness to the outcast, his poverty and other ways in which he showed his self-sacrificing love. The contemplation of these mysteries, as Saint Ignatius of Loyola pointed out, leads us to incarnate them in our choices and attitudes.[18] Because "everything in Jesus' life was a sign of his mystery",[19] "Christ's whole life is a revelation of the Father",[20] "Christ's whole life is a mystery of redemption",[21] "Christ's whole life is a mystery of recapitulation".[22] "Christ enables us to live in him all that he himself lived, and he lives it in us".[23]

21. The Father's plan is Christ, and ourselves in him. In the end, it is Christ who loves in us, for "holiness is

---

[18] *Spiritual Exercises*, 102-312.
[19] Catechism of the Catholic Church, 515.
[20] *Ibid.*, 516.
[21] *Ibid.*, 517.
[22] *Ibid.*, 518.
[23] *Ibid.*, 521.

nothing other than charity lived to the full".[24] As a result, "the measure of our holiness stems from the stature that Christ achieves in us, to the extent that, by the power of the Holy Spirit, we model our whole life on his".[25] Every saint is a message which the Holy Spirit takes from the riches of Jesus Christ and gives to his people.

22. To recognize the word that the Lord wishes to speak to us through one of his saints, we do not need to get caught up in details, for there we might also encounter mistakes and failures. Not everything a saint says is completely faithful to the Gospel; not everything he or she does is authentic or perfect. What we need to contemplate is the totality of their life, their entire journey of growth in holiness, the reflection of Jesus Christ that emerges when we grasp their overall meaning as a person.[26]

23. This is a powerful summons to all of us. You too need to see the entirety of your life as a mission. Try to do so by listening to God in prayer and recognizing the signs that he gives you. Always ask the Spirit what Jesus expects from you at every moment of your life and in every decision you must make, so as to discern its place in the mission you have received. Allow the

[24] Benedict XVI, *Catechesis*, General Audience of 13 April 2011: *Insegnamenti* VII (2011), 451.
[25] *Ibid.*, 450.
[26] Cf. Hans Urs von Balthasar, "Theology and Holiness", in *Communio* 14/4 (1987), 341-350.

Spirit to forge in you the personal mystery that can reflect Jesus Christ in today's world.

24. May you come to realize what that word is, the message of Jesus that God wants to speak to the world by your life. Let yourself be transformed. Let yourself be renewed by the Spirit, so that this can happen, lest you fail in your precious mission. The Lord will bring it to fulfilment despite your mistakes and missteps, provided that you do not abandon the path of love but remain ever open to his supernatural grace, which purifies and enlightens.

ACTIVITY THAT SANCTIFIES

25. Just as you cannot understand Christ apart from the kingdom he came to bring, so too your personal mission is inseparable from the building of that kingdom: "Strive first for the kingdom of God and its righteousness" (Mt 6:33). Your identification with Christ and his will involves a commitment to build with him that kingdom of love, justice and universal peace. Christ himself wants to experience this with you, in all the efforts and sacrifices that it entails, but also in all the joy and enrichment it brings. You cannot grow in holiness without committing yourself, body and soul, to giving your best to this endeavor.

26. It is not healthy to love silence while fleeing interaction with others, to want peace and quiet while avoiding activity, to seek prayer while disdaining service.

Everything can be accepted and integrated into our life in this world, and become a part of our path to holiness. We are called to be contemplatives even in the midst of action, and to grow in holiness by responsibly and generously carrying out our proper mission.

27. Could the Holy Spirit urge us to carry out a mission and then ask us to abandon it, or not fully engage in it, so as to preserve our inner peace? Yet there are times when we are tempted to relegate pastoral engagement or commitment in the world to second place, as if these were "distractions" along the path to growth in holiness and interior peace. We can forget that "life does not have a mission, but is a mission".[27]

28. Needless to say, anything done out of anxiety, pride or the need to impress others will not lead to holiness. We are challenged to show our commitment in such a way that everything we do has evangelical meaning and identifies us all the more with Jesus Christ. We often speak, for example, of the spirituality of the catechist, the spirituality of the diocesan priesthood, the spirituality of work. For the same reason, in *Evangelii Gaudium* I concluded by speaking of a spirituality of mission, in *Laudato Si'* of an ecological spirituality, and in *Amoris Laetitia* of a spirituality of family life.

29. This does not mean ignoring the need for moments of quiet, solitude and silence before God. Quite the contrary. The presence of constantly new

[27] Xavier Zubiri, *Naturaleza, historia, Dios*, Madrid, 1993³, 427.

gadgets, the excitement of travel and an endless array of consumer goods at times leave no room for God's voice to be heard. We are overwhelmed by words, by superficial pleasures and by an increasing din, filled not by joy but rather by the discontent of those whose lives have lost meaning. How can we fail to realize the need to stop this rat race and to recover the personal space needed to carry on a heartfelt dialogue with God? Finding that space may prove painful but it is always fruitful. Sooner or later, we have to face our true selves and let the Lord enter. This may not happen unless "we see ourselves staring into the abyss of a frightful temptation, or have the dizzying sensation of standing on the precipice of utter despair, or find ourselves completely alone and abandoned".[28] In such situations, we find the deepest motivation for living fully our commitment to our work.

30. The same distractions that are omnipresent in today's world also make us tend to absolutize our free time, so that we can give ourselves over completely to the devices that provide us with entertainment or ephemeral pleasures.[29] As a result, we come to resent our mission, our commitment grows slack, and our generous and ready spirit of service begins to flag. This denatures our spiritual experience. Can any spiritual

[28] Carlo M. Martini, *Le confessioni di Pietro*, Cinisello Balsamo, 2017, 69.
[29] We need to distinguish between this kind of superficial entertainment and a healthy culture of leisure, which opens us to others and to reality itself in a spirit of openness and contemplation.

fervor be sound when it dwells alongside sloth in evangelization or in service to others?

31. We need a spirit of holiness capable of filling both our solitude and our service, our personal life and our evangelizing efforts, so that every moment can be an expression of self-sacrificing love in the Lord's eyes. In this way, every minute of our lives can be a step along the path to growth in holiness.

More alive, more human

32. Do not be afraid of holiness. It will take away none of your energy, vitality or joy. On the contrary, you will become what the Father had in mind when he created you, and you will be faithful to your deepest self. To depend on God sets us free from every form of enslavement and leads us to recognize our great dignity. We see this in Saint Josephine Bakhita: "Abducted and sold into slavery at the tender age of seven, she suffered much at the hands of cruel masters. But she came to understand the profound truth that God, and not man, is the true Master of every human being, of every human life. This experience became a source of great wisdom for this humble daughter of Africa".[30]

33. To the extent that each Christian grows in holiness, he or she will bear greater fruit for our world.

[30] John Paul II, Homily at the Mass of Canonization (1 October 2000), 5: AAS 92 (2000), 852.

The bishops of West Africa have observed that "we are being called in the spirit of the New Evangelization to be evangelized and to evangelize through the empowering of all you, the baptized, to take up your roles as salt of the earth and light of the world wherever you find yourselves".[31]

34. Do not be afraid to set your sights higher, to allow yourself to be loved and liberated by God. Do not be afraid to let yourself be guided by the Holy Spirit. Holiness does not make you less human, since it is an encounter between your weakness and the power of God's grace. For in the words of León Bloy, when all is said and done, "the only great tragedy in life, is not to become a saint".[32]

---

[31] Regional Episcopal Conference of West Africa, Pastoral Message at the End of the Second Plenary Assembly, 29 February 2016, 2.

[32] *La femme pauvre*, Paris, 1897, II, 27, p. 388.

CHAPTER TWO

TWO SUBTLE ENEMIES
OF HOLINESS

35. Here I would like to mention two false forms of holiness that can lead us astray: gnosticism and pelagianism. They are two heresies from early Christian times, yet they continue to plague us. In our times too, many Christians, perhaps without realizing it, can be seduced by these deceptive ideas, which reflect an anthropocentric immanentism disguised as Catholic truth.[33] Let us take a look at these two forms of doctrinal or disciplinary security that give rise "to a narcissistic and authoritarian elitism, whereby instead of evangelizing, one analyses and classifies others, and instead of opening the door to grace, one exhausts his or her energies in inspecting and verifying. In neither case is one really concerned about Jesus Christ or others".[34]

---

[33] Cf. Congregation for the Doctrine of the Faith, Letter *Placuit Deo* on Certain Aspects of Christian Salvation (22 February 2018), 4, in *L'Osservatore Romano*, 2 March 2018, pp. 4-5: "Both neo-Pelagian individualism and the neo-Gnostic disregard of the body deface the confession of faith in Christ, the one, universal Savior". This document provides the doctrinal bases for understanding Christian salvation in reference to contemporary neo-gnostic and neo-pelagian tendencies.
[34] Apostolic Exhortation *Evangelii Gaudium* (24 November 2013), 94: AAS 105 (2013), 1060.

36. Gnosticism presumes "a purely subjective faith whose only interest is a certain experience or a set of ideas and bits of information which are meant to console and enlighten, but which ultimately keep one imprisoned in his or her own thoughts and feelings".[35]

An intellect without God and without flesh

37 Thanks be to God, throughout the history of the Church it has always been clear that a person's perfection is measured not by the information or knowledge they possess, but by the depth of their charity. "Gnostics" do not understand this, because they judge others based on their ability to understand the complexity of certain doctrines. They think of the intellect as separate from the flesh, and thus become incapable of touching Christ's suffering flesh in others, locked up as they are in an encyclopedia of abstractions. In the end, by disembodying the mystery, they prefer "a God without Christ, a Christ without the Church, a Church without her people".[36]

38. Certainly this is a superficial conceit: there is much movement on the surface, but the mind is neither deeply moved nor affected. Still, gnosticism exercises a deceptive attraction for some people, since

[35] *Ibid.*: AAS 105 (2013), 1059.
[36] Homily at Mass in Casa Santa Marta, 11 November 2016: *L'Osservatore Romano*, 12 November 2016, p. 8.

the gnostic approach is strict and allegedly pure, and can appear to possess a certain harmony or order that encompasses everything.

39 Here we have to be careful. I am not referring to a rationalism inimical to Christian faith. It can be present within the Church, both among the laity in parishes and teachers of philosophy and theology in centers of formation. Gnostics think that their explanations can make the entirety of the faith and the Gospel perfectly comprehensible. They absolutize their own theories and force others to submit to their way of thinking. A healthy and humble use of reason in order to reflect on the theological and moral teaching of the Gospel is one thing. It is another to reduce Jesus' teaching to a cold and harsh logic that seeks to dominate everything.[37]

A doctrine without mystery

40. Gnosticism is one of the most sinister ideologies because, while unduly exalting knowledge or a specific experience, it considers its own vision of reality to be perfect. Thus, perhaps without even realizing it, this

---

[37] As Saint Bonaventure teaches, "we must suspend all the operations of the mind and we must transform the peak of our affections, directing them to God alone… Since nature can achieve nothing and personal effort very little, it is necessary to give little importance to investigation and much to unction, little to speech and much to interior joy, little to words or writing but all to the gift of God, namely the Holy Spirit, little or no importance should be given to the creature, but all to the Creator, the Father and the Son and the Holy Spirit": Bonaventure, *Itinerarium Mentis in Deum*, VII, 4-5.

ideology feeds on itself and becomes even more myopic. It can become all the more illusory when it masks itself as a disembodied spirituality. For gnosticism "by its very nature seeks to domesticate the mystery",[38] whether the mystery of God and his grace, or the mystery of others' lives.

41. When somebody has an answer for every question, it is a sign that they are not on the right road. They may well be false prophets, who use religion for their own purposes, to promote their own psychological or intellectual theories. God infinitely transcends us; he is full of surprises. We are not the ones to determine when and how we will encounter him; the exact times and places of that encounter are not up to us. Someone who wants everything to be clear and sure presumes to control God's transcendence.

42. Nor can we claim to say where God is not, because God is mysteriously present in the life of every person, in a way that he himself chooses, and we cannot exclude this by our presumed certainties. Even when someone's life appears completely wrecked, even when we see it devastated by vices or addictions, God is present there. If we let ourselves be guided by the Spirit rather than our own preconceptions, we can and must try to find the Lord in every human life. This

[38] Cf. Letter to the Grand Chancellor of the Pontifical Catholic University of Argentina for the Centenary of the Founding of the Faculty of Theology (3 March 2015): *L'Osservatore Romano*, 9-10 March 2015, p. 6.

is part of the mystery that a gnostic mentality cannot accept, since it is beyond its control.

The limits of reason

43. It is not easy to grasp the truth that we have received from the Lord. And it is even more difficult to express it. So we cannot claim that our way of understanding this truth authorizes us to exercise a strict supervision over others' lives. Here I would note that in the Church there legitimately coexist different ways of interpreting many aspects of doctrine and Christian life; in their variety, they "help to express more clearly the immense riches of God's word". It is true that "for those who long for a monolithic body of doctrine guarded by all and leaving no room for nuance, this might appear as undesirable and leading to confusion".[39] Indeed, some currents of gnosticism scorned the concrete simplicity of the Gospel and attempted to replace the trinitarian and incarnate God with a superior Unity, wherein the rich diversity of our history disappeared.

44. In effect, doctrine, or better, our understanding and expression of it, "is not a closed system, devoid of the dynamic capacity to pose questions, doubts, inquiries… The questions of our people, their suffering, their struggles, their dreams, their trials and their worries, all possess an interpretational value that we

[39] Apostolic Exhortation *Evangelii Gaudium* (24 November 2013), 40: AAS 105 (2013), 1037.

cannot ignore if we want to take the principle of the incarnation seriously. Their wondering helps us to wonder, their questions question us".[40]

45. A dangerous confusion can arise. We can think that because we know something, or are able to explain it in certain terms, we are already saints, perfect and better than the "ignorant masses". Saint John Paul II warned of the temptation on the part of those in the Church who are more highly educated "to feel somehow superior to other members of the faithful".[41] In point of fact, what we think we know should always motivate us to respond more fully to God's love. Indeed, "you learn so as to live: theology and holiness are inseparable".[42]

46. When Saint Francis of Assisi saw that some of his disciples were engaged in teaching, he wanted to avoid the temptation to gnosticism. He wrote to Saint Anthony of Padua: "I am pleased that you teach sacred theology to the brothers, provided that… you do not extinguish the spirit of prayer and devotion during study of this kind".[43] Francis recognized the tempta-

---

[40] Video Message to Participants in an International Theological Congress held at the Pontifical Catholic University of Argentina (1-3 September 2015): AAS 107 (2015), 980.

[41] Post-Synodal Apostolic Exhortation *Vita Consecrata* (25 March 1996), 38: AAS 88 (1996), 412.

[42] *Letter to the Grand Chancellor of the Pontifical Catholic University of Argentina for the Centenary of the Founding of the Faculty of Theology* (3 March 2015): L'Osservatore Romano, 9-10 March 2015, p. 6.

[43] *Letter to Brother Anthony*, 2: FF 251.

tion to turn the Christian experience into a set of intellectual exercises that distance us from the freshness of the Gospel. Saint Bonaventure, on the other hand, pointed out that true Christian wisdom can never be separated from mercy towards our neighbor: "The greatest possible wisdom is to share fruitfully what we have to give... Even as mercy is the companion of wisdom, avarice is its enemy".[44] "There are activities that, united to contemplation, do not prevent the latter, but rather facilitate it, such as works of mercy and devotion".[45]

CONTEMPORARY PELAGIANISM

47. Gnosticism gave way to another heresy, likewise present in our day. As time passed, many came to realize that it is not knowledge that betters us or makes us saints, but the kind of life we lead. But this subtly led back to the old error of the gnostics, which was simply transformed rather than eliminated.

48. The same power that the gnostics attributed to the intellect, others now began to attribute to the human will, to personal effort. This was the case with the pelagians and semi-pelagians. Now it was not intelligence that took the place of mystery and grace, but our human will. It was forgotten that everything "depends not on human will or exertion, but on God

[44] *De septem donis*, 9, 15.
[45] *In IV Sent.* 37, 1, 3, ad 6.

who shows mercy" (*Rom* 9:16) and that "he first loved us" (cf. *1 Jn* 4:19).

A will lacking humility

49. Those who yield to this pelagian or semi-pelagian mindset, even though they speak warmly of God's grace, "ultimately trust only in their own powers and feel superior to others because they observe certain rules or remain intransigently faithful to a particular Catholic style".[46] When some of them tell the weak that all things can be accomplished with God's grace, deep down they tend to give the idea that all things are possible by the human will, as if it were something pure, perfect, all-powerful, to which grace is then added. They fail to realize that "not everyone can do everything",[47] and that in this life human weaknesses are not healed completely and once for all by grace.[48] In every case, as Saint Augustine taught, God commands you to do what you can and to ask for what you cannot,[49] and indeed to pray to him humbly: "Grant what you command, and command what you will".[50]

---

[46] Apostolic Exhortation *Evangelii Gaudium* (24 November 2013), 94: AAS 105 (2013), 1059.

[47] Cf. Bonaventure, *De sex alis Seraphim*, 3, 8: "*Non omnes omnia possunt*". The phrase is to be understood along the lines of the Catechism of the Catholic Church, 1735.

[48] Cf. Thomas Aquinas, *Summa Theologiae* I-II, q. 109, a. 9, ad 1: "But here grace is to some extent imperfect, inasmuch as it does not completely heal man, as we have said".

[49] Cf. *De natura et gratia*, 43, 50: PL 44, 271.

[50] *Confessiones*, X, 29, 40: PL 32, 796.

50. Ultimately, the lack of a heartfelt and prayerful acknowledgment of our limitations prevents grace from working more effectively within us, for no room is left for bringing about the potential good that is part of a sincere and genuine journey of growth.[51] Grace, precisely because it builds on nature, does not make us superhuman all at once. That kind of thinking would show too much confidence in our own abilities. Underneath our orthodoxy, our attitudes might not correspond to our talk about the need for grace, and in specific situations we can end up putting little trust in it. Unless we can acknowledge our concrete and limited situation, we will not be able to see the real and possible steps that the Lord demands of us at every moment, once we are attracted and empowered by his gift. Grace acts in history; ordinarily it takes hold of us and transforms us progressively.[52] If we reject this historical and progressive reality, we can actually refuse and block grace, even as we extol it by our words.

51. When God speaks to Abraham, he tells him: "I am God Almighty, walk before me, and be blameless" (*Gen* 17:1). In order to be blameless, as he would have us, we need to live humbly in his presence, cloaked in his glory; we need to walk in union with him, recognizing his constant love in our lives. We need to lose

---

[51] Cf. Apostolic Exhortation *Evangelii Gaudium* (24 November 2013), 44: AAS 105 (2013), 1038.

[52] In the understanding of Christian faith, grace precedes, accompanies and follows all our actions (cf. ecumenical council of Trent, Session VI, *Decree on Justification*, ch. 5: DH 1525).

our fear before that presence which can only be for our good. God is the Father who gave us life and loves us greatly. Once we accept him, and stop trying to live our lives without him, the anguish of loneliness will disappear (cf. *Ps* 139:23-24). In this way we will know the pleasing and perfect will of the Lord (cf. *Rom* 12:1-2) and allow him to mold us like a potter (cf. *Is* 29:16). So often we say that God dwells in us, but it is better to say that we dwell in him, that he enables us to dwell in his light and love. He is our temple; we ask to dwell in the house of the Lord all the days of our life (cf. *Ps* 27:4). "For one day in your courts is better than a thousand elsewhere" (*Ps* 84:10). In him is our holiness.

An often overlooked Church teaching

52. The Church has repeatedly taught that we are justified not by our own works or efforts, but by the grace of the Lord, who always takes the initiative. The Fathers of the Church, even before Saint Augustine, clearly expressed this fundamental belief. Saint John Chrysostom said that God pours into us the very source of all his gifts even before we enter into battle.[53] Saint Basil the Great remarked that the faithful glory in God alone, for "they realize that they lack true justice and are justified only through faith in Christ".[54]

53. The Second Synod of Orange taught with firm authority that nothing human can demand, merit or

[53] Cf. *In Ep. ad Romanos*, 9, 11: PG 60, 470.
[54] *Homilia de Humilitate*: PG 31, 530.

buy the gift of divine grace, and that all cooperation with it is a prior gift of that same grace: "Even the desire to be cleansed comes about in us through the outpouring and working of the Holy Spirit".[55] Subsequently, the Council of Trent, while emphasizing the importance of our cooperation for spiritual growth, reaffirmed that dogmatic teaching: "We are said to be justified gratuitously because nothing that precedes justification, neither faith nor works, merits the grace of justification; for 'if it is by grace, it is no longer on the basis of works; otherwise, grace would no longer be grace' (*Rom* 11:6)".[56]

54. The Catechism of the Catholic Church also reminds us that the gift of grace "surpasses the power of human intellect and will"[57] and that "with regard to God, there is no strict right to any merit on the part of man. Between God and us there is an immeasurable inequality".[58] His friendship infinitely transcends us; we cannot buy it with our works, it can only be a gift born of his loving initiative. This invites us to live in joyful gratitude for this completely unmerited gift, since "after one has grace, the grace already possessed cannot come under merit".[59] The saints avoided putting trust in their own works: "In the evening of this life, I shall appear before you empty-handed, for I do

[55] Canon 4: DH 374.
[56] Session VI, *Decree on Justification*, ch. 8: DH 1532.
[57] No. 1998.
[58] *Ibid.*, 2007.
[59] Thomas Aquinas, *Summa Theologiae*, I-II, q. 114, a. 5.

not ask you, Lord, to count my works. All our justices have stains in your sight".[60]

55. This is one of the great convictions that the Church has come firmly to hold. It is so clearly expressed in the word of God that there can be no question of it. Like the supreme commandment of love, this truth should affect the way we live, for it flows from the heart of the Gospel and demands that we not only accept it intellectually but also make it a source of contagious joy. Yet we cannot celebrate this free gift of the Lord's friendship unless we realize that our earthly life and our natural abilities are his gift. We need "to acknowledge jubilantly that our life is essentially a gift, and recognize that our freedom is a grace. This is not easy today, in a world that thinks it can keep something for itself, the fruits of its own creativity or freedom".[61]

56. Only on the basis of God's gift, freely accepted and humbly received, can we cooperate by our own efforts in our progressive transformation.[62] We must first belong to God, offering ourselves to him who was there first, and entrusting to him our abilities, our

---

[60] Thérèse of the Child Jesus, "Act of Offering to Merciful Love" (Prayers, 6).

[61] Lucio Gera, *Sobre el misterio del pobre*, in P. Grelot-L. Gera-a. Dumas, *El Pobre*, Buenos Aires, 1962, 103.

[62] This is, in a word, the Catholic doctrine on "merit" subsequent to justification: it has to do with the cooperation of the justified for growth in the life of grace (cf. Catechism of the Catholic Church, 2010). Yet this cooperation in no way makes justification itself or friendship with God the object of human merit.

efforts, our struggle against evil and our creativity, so that his free gift may grow and develop within us: "I appeal to you, therefore, brethren, by the mercies of God, to present your bodies as a living sacrifice, holy and acceptable to God" (*Rom* 12:1). For that matter, the Church has always taught that charity alone makes growth in the life of grace possible, for "if I do not have love, I am nothing" (*1 Cor* 13:2).

New pelagians

57. Still, some Christians insist on taking another path, that of justification by their own efforts, the worship of the human will and their own abilities. The result is a self-centered and elitist complacency, bereft of true love. This finds expression in a variety of apparently unconnected ways of thinking and acting: an obsession with the law, an absorption with social and political advantages, a punctilious concern for the Church's liturgy, doctrine and prestige, a vanity about the ability to manage practical matters, and an excessive concern with programs of self-help and personal fulfilment. Some Christians spend their time and energy on these things, rather than letting themselves be led by the Spirit in the way of love, rather than being passionate about communicating the beauty and the joy of the Gospel and seeking out the lost among the immense crowds that thirst for Christ.[63]

---

[63] Cf. Apostolic Exhortation *Evangelii Gaudium* (24 November 2013), 95: AAS 105 (2013), 1060.

58. Not infrequently, contrary to the promptings of the Spirit, the life of the Church can become a museum piece or the possession of a select few. This can occur when some groups of Christians give excessive importance to certain rules, customs or ways of acting. The Gospel then tends to be reduced and constricted, deprived of its simplicity, allure and savor. This may well be a subtle form of pelagianism, for it appears to subject the life of grace to certain human structures. It can affect groups, movements and communities, and it explains why so often they begin with an intense life in the Spirit, only to end up fossilized… or corrupt.

59. Once we believe that everything depends on human effort as channeled by ecclesial rules and structures, we unconsciously complicate the Gospel and become enslaved to a blueprint that leaves few openings for the working of grace. Saint Thomas Aquinas reminded us that the precepts added to the Gospel by the Church should be imposed with moderation "lest the conduct of the faithful become burdensome", for then our religion would become a form of servitude.[64]

The summation of the Law

60. To avoid this, we do well to keep reminding ourselves that there is a hierarchy of virtues that bids us seek what is essential. The primacy belongs to the

---

[64] *Summa Theologiae* I-II, q. 107, art. 4.

theological virtues, which have God as their object and motive. At the center is charity. Saint Paul says that what truly counts is "faith working through love" (*Gal* 5:6). We are called to make every effort to preserve charity: "The one who loves another has fulfilled the law... for love is the fulfilment of the law" (*Rom* 13:8.10). "For the whole law is summed up in a single commandment, 'You shall love your neighbor as yourself'" (*Gal* 5:14).

61. In other words, amid the thicket of precepts and prescriptions, Jesus clears a way to seeing two faces, that of the Father and that of our brother. He does not give us two more formulas or two more commands. He gives us two faces, or better yet, one alone: the face of God reflected in so many other faces. For in every one of our brothers and sisters, especially the least, the most vulnerable, the defenseless and those in need, God's very image is found. Indeed, with the scraps of this frail humanity, the Lord will shape his final work of art. For "what endures, what has value in life, what riches do not disappear? Surely these two: the Lord and our neighbor. These two riches do not disappear!"[65]

62. May the Lord set the Church free from these new forms of gnosticism and pelagianism that weigh her down and block her progress along the path to

[65] Francis, *Homily at Mass for the Jubilee of Socially Excluded People* (13 November 2016): *L'Osservatore Romano*, 14-15 November 2016, p. 8.

holiness! These aberrations take various shapes, according to the temperament and character of each person. So I encourage everyone to reflect and discern before God whether they may be present in their lives.

CHAPTER THREE

IN THE LIGHT
OF THE MASTER

63. There can be any number of theories about what constitutes holiness, with various explanations and distinctions. Such reflection may be useful, but nothing is more enlightening than turning to Jesus' words and seeing his way of teaching the truth. Jesus explained with great simplicity what it means to be holy when he gave us the Beatitudes (cf. *Mt* 5:3-12; *Lk* 6:20-23). The Beatitudes are like a Christian's identity card. So if anyone asks: "What must one do to be a good Christian?", the answer is clear. We have to do, each in our own way, what Jesus told us in the Sermon on the Mount.[66] In the Beatitudes, we find a portrait of the Master, which we are called to reflect in our daily lives.

64. The word "happy" or "blessed" thus becomes a synonym for "holy". It expresses the fact that those

---

[66] Cf. *Homily at Mass in Casa Santa Marta*, 9 June 2014: *L'Osservatore Romano*, 10 June 2014, p. 8.

faithful to God and his word, by their self-giving, gain true happiness.

GOING AGAINST THE FLOW

65. Although Jesus' words may strike us as poetic, they clearly run counter to the way things are usually done in our world. Even if we find Jesus' message attractive, the world pushes us towards another way of living. The Beatitudes are in no way trite or un-demanding, quite the opposite. We can only practice them if the Holy Spirit fills us with his power and frees us from our weakness, our selfishness, our compla-cency and our pride.

66. Let us listen once more to Jesus, with all the love and respect that the Master deserves. Let us allow his words to unsettle us, to challenge us and to demand a real change in the way we live. Otherwise, holiness will remain no more than an empty word. We turn now to the individual Beatitudes in the Gospel of Matthew (cf. *Mt* 5:3-12).[67]

"Blessed are the poor in spirit, for theirs is the kingdom of heaven"

67. The Gospel invites us to peer into the depths of our heart, to see where we find our security in life. Usually the rich feel secure in their wealth, and think

[67] The order of the second and third Beatitudes varies in accordance with the different textual traditions.

that, if that wealth is threatened, the whole meaning of their earthly life can collapse. Jesus himself tells us this in the parable of the rich fool: he speaks of a man who was sure of himself, yet foolish, for it did not dawn on him that he might die that very day (cf. *Lk* 12:16-21).

68. Wealth ensures nothing. Indeed, once we think we are rich, we can become so self-satisfied that we leave no room for God's word, for the love of our brothers and sisters, or for the enjoyment of the most important things in life. In this way, we miss out on the greatest treasure of all. That is why Jesus calls blessed those who are poor in spirit, those who have a poor heart, for there the Lord can enter with his perennial newness.

69. This spiritual poverty is closely linked to what Saint Ignatius of Loyola calls "holy indifference", which brings us to a radiant interior freedom: "We need to train ourselves to be indifferent in our attitude to all created things, in all that is permitted to our free will and not forbidden; so that on our part, we do not set our hearts on good health rather than bad, riches rather than poverty, honor rather than dishonor, a long life rather than a short one, and so in all the rest".[68]

70. Luke does not speak of poverty "of spirit" but simply of those who are "poor" (cf. *Lk* 6:20). In this way, he too invites us to live a plain and austere life. He calls us to share in the life of those most in need,

---

[68] *Spiritual Exercises*, 23d.

the life lived by the Apostles, and ultimately to config-
ure ourselves to Jesus who, though rich, "made himself poor" (2 Cor 8:9). Being poor of heart: that is
holiness.

"Blessed are the meek, for they will inherit the earth"

71. These are strong words in a world that from the
beginning has been a place of conflict, disputes and
enmity on all sides, where we constantly pigeon-
hole others on the basis of their ideas, their customs and even their way of speaking or dressing.
Ultimately, it is the reign of pride and vanity, where
each person thinks he or she has the right to dominate others. Nonetheless, impossible as it may seem,
Jesus proposes a different way of doing things: the
way of meekness. This is what we see him doing
with his disciples. It is what we contemplate on his
entrance to Jerusalem: "Behold, your king is coming to you, humble, and mounted on a donkey"
(Mt 21:5; Zech 9:9).

72. Christ says: "Learn from me; for I am gentle and
humble of heart, and you will find rest for your souls"
(Mt 11:29). If we are constantly upset and impatient
with others, we will end up drained and weary. But if
we regard the faults and limitations of others with
tenderness and meekness, without an air of superior-
ity, we can actually help them and stop wasting our
energy on useless complaining. Saint Thérèse of
Lisieux tells us that "perfect charity consists in putting

up with others' mistakes, and not being scandalized by their faults".[69]

73. Paul speaks of meekness as one of the fruits of the Holy Spirit (cf. *Gal* 5:23). He suggests that, if a wrongful action of one of our brothers or sisters troubles us, we should try to correct them, but "with a spirit of meekness", since "you too could be tempted" (*Gal* 6:1). Even when we defend our faith and convictions, we are to do so "with meekness" (cf. *1 Pet* 3:16). Our enemies too are to be treated "with meekness" (*2 Tim* 2:25). In the Church we have often erred by not embracing this demand of God's word.

74. Meekness is yet another expression of the interior poverty of those who put their trust in God alone. Indeed, in the Bible the same word – *anawim* – usually refers both to the poor and to the meek. Someone might object: "If I am that meek, they will think that I am an idiot, a fool or a weakling". At times they may, but so be it. It is always better to be meek, for then our deepest desires will be fulfilled. The meek "shall inherit the earth", for they will see God's promises accomplished in their lives. In every situation, the meek put their hope in the Lord, and those who hope for him shall possess the land… and enjoy the fullness of peace (cf. *Ps* 37:9.11). For his part, the Lord trusts in them: "This is the one to whom I will look, to the humble and contrite in spirit, who trembles at my word" (*Is* 66:2).

[69] *Manuscript* C, 12r.

Reacting with meekness and humility: that is holiness.

"Blessed are those who mourn, for they will be comforted"

75. The world tells us exactly the opposite: entertainment, pleasure, diversion and escape make for the good life. The worldly person ignores problems of sickness or sorrow in the family or all around him; he averts his gaze. The world has no desire to mourn; it would rather disregard painful situations, cover them up or hide them. Much energy is expended on fleeing from situations of suffering in the belief that reality can be concealed. But the cross can never be absent.

76. A person who sees things as they truly are and sympathizes with pain and sorrow is capable of touching life's depths and finding authentic happiness.[70] He or she is consoled, not by the world but by Jesus. Such persons are unafraid to share in the suffering of others; they do not flee from painful situations. They discover the meaning of life by coming to the aid of those who suffer, understanding their anguish and bringing relief. They sense that the other is flesh of our flesh, and are not afraid to draw near, even to touch their wounds. They feel compassion for others in such a

---

[70] From the patristic era, the Church has valued the gift of tears, as seen in the fine prayer *"Ad petendam compunctionem cordis"*. It reads: "Almighty and most merciful God, who brought forth from the rock a spring of living water for your thirsting people: bring forth tears of compunction from our hardness of heart, that we may grieve for our sins, and, by your mercy, obtain their forgiveness" (cf. *Missale Romanum*, ed. typ. 1962, p. [110]).

way that all distance vanishes. In this way they can embrace Saint Paul's exhortation: "Weep with those who weep" (*Rom* 12:15).

Knowing how to mourn with others: that is holiness.

"Blessed are those who hunger and thirst for righteousness, for they will be filled"

77. Hunger and thirst are intense experiences, since they involve basic needs and our instinct for survival. There are those who desire justice and yearn for righteousness with similar intensity. Jesus says that they will be satisfied, for sooner or later justice will come. We can cooperate to make that possible, even if we may not always see the fruit of our efforts.

78. Jesus offers a justice other than that of the world, so often marred by petty interests and manipulated in various ways. Experience shows how easy it is to become mired in corruption, ensnared in the daily politics of *quid pro quo*, where everything becomes business. How many people suffer injustice, standing by powerlessly while others divvy up the good things of this life. Some give up fighting for real justice and opt to follow in the train of the winners. This has nothing to do with the hunger and thirst for justice that Jesus praises.

79. True justice comes about in people's lives when they themselves are just in their decisions; it is expressed in their pursuit of justice for the poor and the weak.

While it is true that the word "justice" can be a synonym for faithfulness to God's will in every aspect of our life, if we give the word too general a meaning, we forget that it is shown especially in justice towards those who are most vulnerable: "Seek justice, correct oppression; defend the fatherless, plead for the widow" (*Is* 1:17).

Hungering and thirsting for righteousness: that is holiness.

"Blessed are the merciful, for they will receive mercy"

80. Mercy has two aspects. It involves giving, helping and serving others, but it also includes forgiveness and understanding. Matthew sums it up in one golden rule: "In everything, do to others as you would have them do to you" (7:12). The Catechism reminds us that this law is to be applied "in every case",[71] especially when we are "confronted by situations that make moral judgments less assured and decision difficult".[72]

81. Giving and forgiving means reproducing in our lives some small measure of God's perfection, which gives and forgives superabundantly. For this reason, in the Gospel of Luke we do not hear the words, "Be perfect" (*Mt* 5:48), but rather, "Be merciful, even as your Father is merciful. Judge not, and you will not be judged;

---

[71] Catechism of the Catholic Church, 1789; cf. 1970.
[72] *Ibid.*, 1787.

condemn not, and you will not be condemned; forgive, and you will be forgiven; give, and it will be given to you" (6:36-38). Luke then adds something not to be overlooked: "The measure you give will be the measure you get back" (6:38). The yardstick we use for understanding and forgiving others will measure the forgiveness we receive. The yardstick we use for giving will measure what we receive. We should never forget this.

82 Jesus does not say, "Blessed are those who plot revenge". He calls "blessed" those who forgive and do so "seventy times seven" (*Mt* 18:22). We need to think of ourselves as an army of the forgiven. All of us have been looked upon with divine compassion. If we approach the Lord with sincerity and listen carefully, there may well be times when we hear his reproach: "Should not you have had mercy on your fellow servant, as I had mercy on you?" (*Mt* 18:33).

Seeing and acting with mercy: that is holiness.

"Blessed are the pure in heart, for they will see God"

83. This Beatitude speaks of those whose hearts are simple, pure and undefiled, for a heart capable of love admits nothing that might harm, weaken or endanger that love. The Bible uses the heart to describe our real intentions, the things we truly seek and desire, apart from all appearances. "Man sees the appearance, but the Lord looks into the heart" (*1 Sam* 16:7). God wants to speak to our hearts (cf. *Hos* 2:16); there he desires to write his law (cf. *Jer* 31:33). In a word, he wants to give us a new heart (cf. *Ezek* 36:26).

84. "Guard your heart with all vigilance" (*Prov* 4:23). Nothing stained by falsehood has any real worth in the Lord's eyes. He "flees from deceit, and rises and departs from foolish thoughts" (*Wis* 1:5). The Father, "who sees in secret" (*Mt* 6:6), recognizes what is impure and insincere, mere display or appearance, as does the Son, who knows "what is in man" (cf. *Jn* 2:25).

85. Certainly there can be no love without works of love, but this Beatitude reminds us that the Lord expects a commitment to our brothers and sisters that comes from the heart. For "if I give away all I have, and if I deliver my body to be burned, but have no love, I gain nothing" (*1 Cor* 13:3). In Matthew's Gospel too, we see that what proceeds from the heart is what defiles a person (cf. 15:18), for from the heart come murder, theft, false witness, and other evil deeds (cf. 15:19). From the heart's intentions come the desires and the deepest decisions that determine our actions.

86. A heart that loves God and neighbor (cf. *Mt* 22:36-40), genuinely and not merely in words, is a pure heart; it can see God. In his hymn to charity, Saint Paul says that "now we see in a mirror, dimly" (*1 Cor* 13:12), but to the extent that truth and love prevail, we will then be able to see "face to face". Jesus promises that those who are pure in heart "will see God".

Keeping a heart free of all that tarnishes love: that is holiness.

"Blessed are the peacemakers, for they will be called children of God"

87. This Beatitude makes us think of the many endless situations of war in our world. Yet we ourselves are often a cause of conflict or at least of misunderstanding. For example, I may hear something about someone and I go off and repeat it. I may even embellish it the second time around and keep spreading it… And the more harm it does, the more satisfaction I seem to derive from it. The world of gossip, inhabited by negative and destructive people, does not bring peace. Such people are really the enemies of peace; in no way are they "blessed".[73]

88. Peacemakers truly "make" peace; they build peace and friendship in society. To those who sow peace Jesus makes this magnificent promise: "They will be called children of God" (*Mt* 5:9). He told his disciples that, wherever they went, they were to say: "Peace to this house!" (*Lk* 10:5). The word of God exhorts every believer to work for peace, "along with all who call upon the Lord with a pure heart" (cf. *2 Tim* 2:22), for "the harvest of righteousness is

---

[73] Detraction and calumny are acts of terrorism: a bomb is thrown, it explodes and the attacker walks away calm and contented. This is completely different from the nobility of those who speak to others face to face, serenely and frankly, out of genuine concern for their good.

sown in peace by those who make peace" (*Jas* 3:18). And if there are times in our community when we question what ought to be done, "let us pursue what makes for peace" (*Rom* 14:19), for unity is preferable to conflict.[74]

89. It is not easy to "make" this evangelical peace, which excludes no one but embraces even those who are a bit odd, troublesome or difficult, demanding, different, beaten down by life or simply uninterested. It is hard work; it calls for great openness of mind and heart, since it is not about creating "a consensus on paper or a transient peace for a contented minority",[75] or a project "by a few for the few".[76] Nor can it attempt to ignore or disregard conflict; instead, it must "face conflict head on, resolve it and make it a link in the chain of a new process".[77] We need to be artisans of peace, for building peace is a craft that demands serenity, creativity, sensitivity and skill.

Sowing peace all around us: that is holiness.

---

[74] At times, it may be necessary to speak of the difficulties of a particular brother or sister. In such cases, it can happen that an interpretation is passed on in place of an objective fact. Emotions can misconstrue and alter the facts of a matter, and end up passing them on laced with subjective elements. In this way, neither the facts themselves nor the truth of the other person are respected.

[75] Apostolic Exhortation, *Evangelii Gaudium* (24 November 2013), 218: AAS 105 (2013), 1110.

[76] *Ibid.*, 239: 1116.

[77] *Ibid.*, 227: 1112.

"Blessed are those who are persecuted for righteousness' sake, for theirs is the kingdom of heaven"

90. Jesus himself warns us that the path he proposes goes against the flow, even making us challenge society by the way we live and, as a result, becoming a nuisance. He reminds us how many people have been, and still are, persecuted simply because they struggle for justice, because they take seriously their commitment to God and to others. Unless we wish to sink into an obscure mediocrity, let us not long for an easy life, for "whoever would save his life will lose it" (*Mt* 16:25).

91. In living the Gospel, we cannot expect that everything will be easy, for the thirst for power and worldly interests often stands in our way. Saint John Paul II noted that "a society is alienated if its forms of social organization, production and consumption make it more difficult to offer this gift of self and to establish this solidarity between people".[78] In such a society, politics, mass communications and economic, cultural and even religious institutions become so entangled as to become an obstacle to authentic human and social development. As a result, the Beatitudes are not easy to live out; any attempt to do so will be viewed negatively, regarded with suspicion, and met with ridicule.

[78] Encyclical Letter *Centesimus Annus* (1 May 1991), 41c: *AAS* 81 (1993), 844-845.

92. Whatever weariness and pain we may experience in living the commandment of love and following the way of justice, the cross remains the source of our growth and sanctification. We must never forget that when the New Testament tells us that we will have to endure suffering for the Gospel's sake, it speaks precisely of persecution (cf. *Acts* 5:41; *Phil* 1:29; *Col* 1:24; *2 Tim* 1:12; *1 Pet* 2:20, 4:14, 16; *Rev* 2:10).

93. Here we are speaking about inevitable persecution, not the kind of persecution we might bring upon ourselves by our mistreatment of others. The saints are not odd and aloof, unbearable because of their vanity, negativity and bitterness. The Apostles of Christ were not like that. The Book of Acts states repeatedly that they enjoyed favor "with all the people" (2:47; cf. 4:21, 33; 5:13), even as some authorities harassed and persecuted them (cf. 4:1-3, 5:17-18).

94. Persecutions are not a reality of the past, for today too we experience them, whether by the shedding of blood, as is the case with so many contemporary martyrs, or by more subtle means, by slander and lies. Jesus calls us blessed when people "utter all kinds of evil against you falsely on my account" (*Mt* 5:11). At other times, persecution can take the form of gibes that try to caricature our faith and make us seem ridiculous.

Accepting daily the path of the Gospel, even though it may cause us problems: that is holiness.

95. In the twenty-fifth chapter of Matthew's Gospel (vv. 31-46), Jesus expands on the Beatitude that calls blessed the merciful. If we seek the holiness pleasing to God's eyes, this text offers us one clear criterion on which we will be judged. "I was hungry and you gave me food, I was thirsty and you gave me drink, I was a stranger and you welcomed me, I was naked and you clothed me, I was sick and you took care of me, I was in prison and you visited me" (vv. 35-36).

In fidelity to the Master

96. Holiness, then, is not about swooning in mystic rapture. As Saint John Paul II said: "If we truly start out anew from the contemplation of Christ, we must learn to see him especially in the faces of those with whom he himself wished to be identified".[79] The text of Matthew 25:35-36 is "not a simple invitation to charity: it is a page of Christology which sheds a ray of light on the mystery of Christ".[80] In this call to recognize him in the poor and the suffering, we see revealed the very heart of Christ, his deepest feelings and choices, which every saint seeks to imitate.

97. Given these uncompromising demands of Jesus, it is my duty to ask Christians to acknowledge and accept them in a spirit of genuine openness, *sine glossa*.

[79] Apostolic Letter *Novo Millennio Ineunte* (6 January 2001), 49: AAS 93 (2001), 302.
[80] *Ibid.*

In other words, without any "ifs or buts" that could lessen their force. Our Lord made it very clear that holiness cannot be understood or lived apart from these demands, for mercy is "the beating heart of the Gospel".[81]

98. If I encounter a person sleeping outdoors on a cold night, I can view him or her as an annoyance, an idler, an obstacle in my path, a troubling sight, a problem for politicians to sort out, or even a piece of refuse cluttering a public space. Or I can respond with faith and charity, and see in this person a human being with a dignity identical to my own, a creature infinitely loved by the Father, an image of God, a brother or sister redeemed by Jesus Christ. That is what it is to be a Christian! Can holiness somehow be understood apart from this lively recognition of the dignity of each human being?[82]

99. For Christians, this involves a constant and healthy unease. Even if helping one person alone could justify all our efforts, it would not be enough. The bishops of Canada made this clear when they noted, for example, that the biblical understanding of the jubilee year was about more than simply performing certain good works. It also meant seeking social change: "For later generations to also be released, clearly the goal had to

---

[81] Bull *Misericordiae Vultus* (11 April 2015), 12: AAS 107 (2015), 407.

[82] We can recall the Good Samaritan's reaction upon meeting the man attacked by robbers and left for dead (cf. *Lk* 10:30-37).

be the restoration of just social and economic systems, so there could no longer be exclusion".[83]

Ideologies striking at the heart of the Gospel

100. I regret that ideologies lead us at times to two harmful errors. On the one hand, there is the error of those Christians who separate these Gospel demands from their personal relationship with the Lord, from their interior union with him, from openness to his grace. Christianity thus becomes a sort of NGO stripped of the luminous mysticism so evident in the lives of Saint Francis of Assisi, Saint Vincent de Paul, Saint Teresa of Calcutta, and many others. For these great saints, mental prayer, the love of God and the reading of the Gospel in no way detracted from their passionate and effective commitment to their neighbors; quite the opposite.

101. The other harmful ideological error is found in those who find suspect the social engagement of others, seeing it as superficial, worldly, secular, materialist, communist or populist. Or they relativize it, as if there are other more important matters, or the only thing that counts is one particular ethical issue or cause that they themselves defend. Our defense of the innocent unborn, for example, needs to be clear, firm and passionate, for at stake is the dignity of a human

[83] Social Affairs Commission of the Canadian Conference of Catholic Bishops, Open Letter to the Members of Parliament, *The Common Good or Exclusion: A Choice for Canadians* (1 February 2001), 9.

life, which is always sacred and demands love for each person, regardless of his or her stage of development. Equally sacred, however, are the lives of the poor, those already born, the destitute, the abandoned and the underprivileged, the vulnerable infirm and elderly exposed to covert euthanasia, the victims of human trafficking, new forms of slavery, and every form of rejection.[84] We cannot uphold an ideal of holiness that would ignore injustice in a world where some revel, spend with abandon and live only for the latest consumer goods, even as others look on from afar, living their entire lives in abject poverty.

102. We often hear it said that, with respect to relativism and the flaws of our present world, the situation of migrants, for example, is a lesser issue. Some Catholics consider it a secondary issue compared to the "grave" bioethical questions. That a politician looking for votes might say such a thing is understandable, but not a Christian, for whom the only proper attitude is to stand in the shoes of those brothers and sisters of ours who risk their lives to offer a future to their children. Can we not realize that this is exactly what Jesus demands of us, when he tells us that in welcoming the stranger we welcome him (cf. *Mt* 25:35)? Saint Benedict did so readily, and though it

[84] The Fifth General Conference of the Latin American and Caribbean Bishops, echoing the Church's constant teaching, stated that human beings "are always sacred, from their conception, at all stages of existence, until their natural death, and after death", and that life must be safeguarded "starting at conception, *in all its stages*, until natural death" (*Aparecida Document*, 29 June 2007, 388; 464).

might have "complicated" the life of his monks, he ordered that all guests who knocked at the monastery door be welcomed "like Christ",[85] with a gesture of veneration;[86] the poor and pilgrims were to be met with "the greatest care and solicitude".[87]

103. A similar approach is found in the Old Testament: "You shall not wrong a stranger or oppress him, for you yourselves were strangers in the land of Egypt" (*Ex* 22:21). "When a stranger resides with you in your land, you shall not oppress him. The stranger who resides with you shall be to you as the citizen among you; and you shall love him as yourself; for you were strangers in the land of Egypt" (*Lev* 19:33-34). This is not a notion invented by some Pope, or a momentary fad. In today's world too, we are called to follow the path of spiritual wisdom proposed by the prophet Isaiah to show what is pleasing to God. "Is it not to share your bread with the hungry and bring the homeless poor into your house; when you see the naked, to cover him, and not to hide yourself from your own kin? Then your light shall break forth like the dawn" (58:7-8).

The worship most acceptable to God

104. We may think that we give glory to God only by our worship and prayer, or simply by following certain ethical norms. It is true that the primacy belongs to

---

[85] *Rule*, 53, 1: PL 66, 749.
[86] Cf. *ibid.*, 53, 7: PL 66, 750.
[87] *Ibid.*, 53, 15: PL 66, 751.

our relationship with God, but we cannot forget that the ultimate criterion on which our lives will be judged is what we have done for others. Prayer is most precious, for it nourishes a daily commitment to love. Our worship becomes pleasing to God when we devote ourselves to living generously, and allow God's gift, granted in prayer, to be shown in our concern for our brothers and sisters.

105. Similarly, the best way to discern if our prayer is authentic is to judge to what extent our life is being transformed in the light of mercy. For "mercy is not only an action of the Father; it becomes a criterion for ascertaining who his true children are".[88] Mercy "is the very foundation of the Church's life".[89] Here I would like to reiterate that mercy does not exclude justice and truth; indeed, "we have to say that mercy is the fullness of justice and the most radiant manifestation of God's truth".[90] It is "the key to heaven".[91]

106. In this regard, I think of Saint Thomas Aquinas, who asked which actions of ours are noblest, which external works best show our love for God. Thomas answered unhesitatingly that they are the works of mercy towards our neighbour,[92] even more than our

---

[88] Bull *Misericordiae Vultus* (11 April 2015), 9: AAS 107 (2015), 405.

[89] *Ibid.*, 10, 406.

[90] Post-Synodal Apostolic Exhortation *Amoris Laetitia* (19 March 2016), 311: AAS 108 (2016), 439.

[91] Apostolic Exhortation *Evangelii Gaudium* (24 November 2013), 197: AAS 105 (2013), 1103.

[92] Cf. *Summa Theologiae*, II-II, q. 30, a. 4.

acts of worship: "We worship God by outward sacrifices and gifts, not for his own benefit, but for that of ourselves and our neighbor. For he does not need our sacrifices, but wishes them to be offered to him, in order to stir our devotion and to profit our neighbor. Hence mercy, whereby we supply others' defects, is a sacrifice more acceptable to him, as conducing more directly to our neighbor's well-being".[93]

107. Those who really wish to give glory to God by their lives, who truly long to grow in holiness, are called to be single-minded and tenacious in their practice of the works of mercy. Saint Teresa of Calcutta clearly realized this: "Yes, I have many human faults and failures... But God bends down and uses us, you and me, to be his love and his compassion in the world; he bears our sins, our troubles and our faults. He depends on us to love the world and to show how much he loves it. If we are too concerned with ourselves, we will have no time left for others".[94]

108. Hedonism and consumerism can prove our downfall, for when we are obsessed with our own pleasure, we end up being all too concerned about ourselves and our rights, and we feel a desperate need for free time to enjoy ourselves. We will find it hard to feel and show any real concern for those in need, unless we are able to cultivate a certain simplicity of

[93] *Ibid.*, ad 1.
[94] Cited in Spanish translation: *Cristo en los Pobres*, Madrid, 1981, 37-38.

life, resisting the feverish demands of a consumer society, which leave us impoverished and unsatisfied, anxious to have it all now. Similarly, when we allow ourselves to be caught up in superficial information, instant communication and virtual reality, we can waste precious time and become indifferent to the suffering flesh of our brothers and sisters. Yet even amid this whirlwind of activity, the Gospel continues to resound, offering us the promise of a different life, a healthier and happier life.

* * *

109. The powerful witness of the saints is revealed in their lives, shaped by the Beatitudes and the criterion of the final judgement. Jesus' words are few and straightforward, yet practical and valid for everyone, for Christianity is meant above all to be put into practice. It can also be an object of study and reflection, but only to help us better live the Gospel in our daily lives. I recommend rereading these great biblical texts frequently, referring back to them, praying with them, trying to embody them. They will benefit us; they will make us genuinely happy.

CHAPTER FOUR

SIGNS OF HOLINESS IN
TODAY'S WORLD

110. Within the framework of holiness offered by the Beatitudes and Matthew 25:31-46, I would like to mention a few signs or spiritual attitudes that, in my opinion, are necessary if we are to understand the way of life to which the Lord calls us. I will not pause to explain the means of sanctification already known to us: the various methods of prayer, the inestimable sacraments of the Eucharist and Reconciliation, the offering of personal sacrifices, different forms of devotion, spiritual direction, and many others as well. Here I will speak only of certain aspects of the call to holiness that I hope will prove especially meaningful.

111. The signs I wish to highlight are not the sum total of a model of holiness, but they are five great expressions of love for God and neighbor that I consider of particular importance in the light of certain dangers and limitations present in today's culture. There we see a sense of anxiety, sometimes violent, that distracts and debilitates; negativity and sullenness; the self-content bred by consumerism; individualism and all those forms of ersatz spirituality – having nothing to do with God – that dominate the current religious marketplace.

PERSEVERANCE, PATIENCE AND MEEKNESS

112. The first of these great signs is solid grounding in the God who loves and sustains us. This source of inner strength enables us to persevere amid life's ups and downs, but also to endure hostility, betrayal and failings on the part of others. "If God is for us, who is against us?" (*Rom* 8:31): this is the source of the peace found in the saints. Such inner strength makes it possible for us, in our fast-paced, noisy and aggressive world, to give a witness of holiness through patience and constancy in doing good. It is a sign of the fidelity born of love, for those who put their faith in God (*pístis*) can also be faithful to others (*pistós*). They do not desert others in bad times; they accompany them in their anxiety and distress, even though doing so may not bring immediate satisfaction.

113. Saint Paul bade the Romans not to repay evil for evil (cf. *Rom* 12:17), not to seek revenge (v. 19), and not to be overcome by evil, but instead to "overcome evil with good" (v. 21). This attitude is not a sign of weakness but of true strength, because God himself "is slow to anger but great in power" (*Nah* 1:3). The word of God exhorts us to "put away all bitterness and wrath and wrangling and slander, together with all malice" (*Eph* 4:31).

114. We need to recognize and combat our aggressive and selfish inclinations, and not let them take root. "Be angry but do not sin; do not let the sun go down on your anger" (*Eph* 4:26). When we feel overwhelmed, we can always cling to the anchor of prayer, which puts us back in God's hands and the source of our peace. "Have no anxiety about anything, but in everything, by prayer and supplication with thanksgiving, let your requests be made known to God. And the peace of God, which surpasses all understanding, will guard your hearts..." (*Phil* 4:6-7).

115. Christians too can be caught up in networks of verbal violence through the internet and the various forums of digital communication. Even in Catholic media, limits can be overstepped, defamation and slander can become commonplace, and all ethical standards and respect for the good name of others can be abandoned. The result is a dangerous dichotomy, since things can be said there that would be unacceptable in public discourse, and people look to compensate for their own discontent by lashing out at others. It is striking that at times, in claiming to uphold the other commandments, they completely ignore the eighth, which forbids bearing false witness or lying, and ruthlessly vilify others. Here we see how the unguarded tongue, set on fire by hell, sets all things ablaze (cf. *Jas* 3:6).

116. Inner strength, as the work of grace, prevents us from becoming carried away by the violence that is so much a part of life today, because grace defuses vanity and makes possible meekness of heart. The saints do not waste energy complaining about the failings of others; they can hold their tongue before the faults of their brothers and sisters, and avoid the verbal violence that demeans and mistreats others. Saints hesitate to treat others harshly; they consider others better than themselves (cf. *Phil* 2:3).

117. It is not good when we look down on others like heartless judges, lording it over them and always trying to teach them lessons. That is itself a subtle form of violence.[95] Saint John of the Cross proposed a different path: "Always prefer to be taught by all, rather than to desire teaching even the least of all".[96] And he added advice on how to keep the devil at bay: "Rejoice in the good of others as if it were your own, and desire that they be given precedence over you in all things; this you should do wholeheartedly. You will thereby overcome evil with good, banish the devil, and possess a happy heart. Try to practice this all the more with those who least attract you. Realize that if you do not train yourself in this way, you will not attain real charity or make any progress in it".[97]

118. Humility can only take root in the heart through humiliations. Without them, there is no humility or holiness. If you are unable to suffer and offer up a few

[95] There are some forms of bullying that, while seeming delicate or respectful and even quite spiritual, cause great damage to others' self-esteem.

[96] *Precautions*, 13.

[97] *Ibid.*, 13.

humiliations, you are not humble and you are not on the path to holiness. The holiness that God bestows on his Church comes through the humiliation of his Son. He is the way. Humiliation makes you resemble Jesus; it is an unavoidable aspect of the imitation of Christ. For "Christ suffered for you, leaving you an example, so that you might follow in his steps" (*1 Pet* 2:21). In turn, he reveals the humility of the Father, who condescends to journey with his people, enduring their infidelities and complaints (cf. *Ex* 34:6-9; *Wis* 11:23-12:2; *Lk* 6:36). For this reason, the Apostles, after suffering humiliation, rejoiced "that they were counted worthy to suffer dishonor for [Jesus'] name" (*Acts* 5:41).

119. Here I am not speaking only about stark situations of martyrdom, but about the daily humiliations of those who keep silent to save their families, who prefer to praise others rather than boast about themselves, or who choose the less welcome tasks, at times even choosing to bear an injustice so as to offer it to the Lord. "If when you do right and suffer for it, you have God's approval" (*1 Pet* 2:20). This does not mean walking around with eyes lowered, not saying a word and fleeing the company of others. At times, precisely because someone is free of selfishness, he or she can dare to disagree gently, to demand justice or to defend the weak before the powerful, even if it may harm his or her reputation.

120. I am not saying that such humiliation is pleasant, for that would be masochism, but that it is a way of imitating Jesus and growing in union with him. This is incomprehensible on a purely natural level, and the world mocks any such notion. Instead, it is a grace to be sought in prayer: "Lord, when humiliations come, help me to know that I am following in your footsteps".

121. To act in this way presumes a heart set at peace by Christ, freed from the aggressiveness born of overweening egotism. That same peacefulness, the fruit of grace, makes it possible to preserve our inner trust and persevere in goodness, "though I walk through the valley of the shadow of death" (*Ps* 23:4) or "a host encamp against me" (*Ps* 27:3). Standing firm in the Lord, the Rock, we can sing: "In peace I will both lie down and sleep; for you alone, O Lord, make me dwell in safety" (*Ps* 4:8). Christ, in a word, "is our peace" (*Eph* 2:14); he came "to guide our feet into the way of peace" (*Lk* 1:79). As he told Saint Faustina Kowalska, "Mankind will not have peace until it turns with trust to my mercy".[98] So let us not fall into the temptation of looking for security in success, vain pleasures, possessions, power over others or social status. Jesus says: "My peace I give to you; I do not give it to you as the world gives peace" (*Jn* 14:27).

JOY AND A SENSE OF HUMOR

122. Far from being timid, morose, acerbic or melancholy, or putting on a dreary face, the saints are joyful

---

[98] Cf. *Diary. Divine Mercy in My Soul*, Stockbridge, 2000, p. 139 (300).

and full of good humor. Though completely realistic, they radiate a positive and hopeful spirit. The Christian life is "joy in the Holy Spirit" (*Rom* 14:17), for "the necessary result of the love of charity is joy; since every lover rejoices at being united to the beloved... the effect of charity is joy".[99] Having received the beautiful gift of God's word, we embrace it "in much affliction, with joy inspired by the Holy Spirit" (*1 Thess* 1:6). If we allow the Lord to draw us out of our shell and change our lives, then we can do as Saint Paul tells us: "Rejoice in the Lord always; I say it again, rejoice!" (*Phil* 4:4).

123. The prophets proclaimed the times of Jesus, in which we now live, as a revelation of joy. "Shout and sing for joy!" (*Is* 12:6). "Get you up to a high mountain, O herald of good tidings to Zion; lift up your voice with strength, O herald of good tidings to Jerusalem!" (*Is* 40:9). "Break forth, O mountains, into singing! For the Lord has comforted his people, and he will have compassion on his afflicted" (*Is* 49:13). "Rejoice greatly, O daughter of Zion! Shout aloud, O daughter of Jerusalem! Behold, your king comes to you; triumphant and victorious is he" (*Zech* 9:9). Nor should we forget Nehemiah's exhortation: "Do not be grieved, for the joy of the Lord is your strength!" (8:10).

124. Mary, recognizing the newness that Jesus brought, sang: "My spirit rejoices" (*Lk* 1:47), and

---

[99] Thomas Aquinas, *Summa Theologiae*, I-II, q. 70, a. 3.

Jesus himself "rejoiced in the Holy Spirit" (*Lk* 10:21). As he passed by, "all the people rejoiced" (*Lk* 13:17). After his resurrection, wherever the disciples went, there was "much joy" (*Acts* 8:8). Jesus assures us: "You will be sorrowful, but your sorrow will turn into joy... I will see you again and your hearts will rejoice, and no one will take your joy from you" (*Jn* 16:20.22). "These things I have spoken to you, that my joy may be in you, and that your joy may be full" (*Jn* 15:11).

125. Hard times may come, when the cross casts its shadow, yet nothing can destroy the supernatural joy that "adapts and changes, but always endures, even as a flicker of light born of our personal certainty that, when everything is said and done, we are infinitely loved".[100] That joy brings deep security, serene hope and a spiritual fulfilment that the world cannot understand or appreciate.

126. Christian joy is usually accompanied by a sense of humor. We see this clearly, for example, in Saint Thomas More, Saint Vincent de Paul and Saint Philip Neri. Ill humor is no sign of holiness. "Remove vexation from your mind" (*Eccl* 11:10). We receive so much from the Lord "for our enjoyment" (*1 Tim* 6:17), that sadness can be a sign of ingratitude. We can get so

---

[100] Apostolic Exhortation *Evangelii Gaudium* (24 November 2013), 6: AAS 105 (2013), 1221.

caught up in ourselves that we are unable to recognize God's gifts.[101]

127. With the love of a father, God tells us: "My son, treat yourself well... Do not deprive yourself of a happy day" (*Sir* 14:11, 14). He wants us to be positive, grateful and uncomplicated: "In the day of prosperity, be joyful... God created human beings straightforward, but they have devised many schemes" (*Eccl* 7:14, 29). Whatever the case, we should remain resilient and imitate Saint Paul: "I have learned to be content with what I have" (*Phil* 4:11). Saint Francis of Assisi lived by this; he could be overwhelmed with gratitude before a piece of hard bread, or joyfully praise God simply for the breeze that caressed his face.

128. This is not the joy held out by today's individualistic and consumerist culture. Consumerism only bloats the heart. It can offer occasional and passing pleasures, but not joy. Here I am speaking of a joy lived in communion, which shares and is shared, since

[101] I recommend praying the prayer attributed to Saint Thomas More: "Grant me, O Lord, good digestion, and also something to digest. Grant me a healthy body, and the necessary good humor to maintain it. Grant me a simple soul that knows to treasure all that is good and that doesn't frighten easily at the sight of evil, but rather finds the means to put things back in their place. Give me a soul that knows not boredom, grumbling, sighs and laments, nor excess of stress, because of that obstructing thing called 'I'. Grant me, O Lord, a sense of good humor. Allow me the grace to be able to take a joke and to discover in life a bit of joy, and to be able to share it with others".

"there is more happiness in giving than in receiving" (*Acts* 20:35) and "God loves a cheerful giver" (*2 Cor* 9:7). Fraternal love increases our capacity for joy, since it makes us capable of rejoicing in the good of others: "Rejoice with those who rejoice" (*Rom* 12:15). "We rejoice when we are weak and you are strong" (*2 Cor* 13:9). On the other hand, when we "focus primarily on our own needs, we condemn ourselves to a joyless existence".[102]

BOLDNESS AND PASSION

129. Holiness is also *parrhesía*: it is boldness, an impulse to evangelize and to leave a mark in this world. To allow us to do this, Jesus himself comes and tells us once more, serenely yet firmly: "Do not be afraid" (*Mk* 6:50). "I am with you always, to the end of the world" (*Mt* 28:20). These words enable us to go forth and serve with the same courage that the Holy Spirit stirred up in the Apostles, impelling them to proclaim Jesus Christ. Boldness, enthusiasm, the freedom to speak out, apostolic fervor, all these are included in the word *parrhesía*. The Bible also uses this word to describe the freedom of a life open to God and to others (cf. *Acts* 4:29, 9:28, 28:31; *2 Cor* 3:12; *Eph* 3:12; *Heb* 3:6, 10:19).

130. Blessed Paul VI, in referring to obstacles to evangelization, spoke of a lack of fervour (*parrhesía*) that

---

[102] Post-Synodal Apostolic Exhortation *Amoris Laetitia* (19 March 2016), 110: AAS 108 (2016), 354.

is "all the more serious because it comes from within".[103] How often we are tempted to keep close to the shore! Yet the Lord calls us to put out into the deep and let down our nets (cf. *Lk* 5:4). He bids us spend our lives in his service. Clinging to him, we are inspired to put all our charisms at the service of others. May we always feel compelled by his love (*2 Cor* 5:14) and say with Saint Paul: "Woe to me if I do not preach the Gospel" (*1 Cor* 9:16).

131. Look at Jesus. His deep compassion reached out to others. It did not make him hesitant, timid or self-conscious, as often happens with us. Quite the opposite. His compassion made him go out actively to preach and to send others on a mission of healing and liberation. Let us acknowledge our weakness, but allow Jesus to lay hold of it and send us too on mission. We are weak, yet we hold a treasure that can enlarge us and make those who receive it better and happier. Boldness and apostolic courage are an essential part of mission.

---

[103] Apostolic Exhortation *Evangelii Nuntiandi* (8 December 1975), 80: AAS 68 (1976), 73. It is worth noting that in this text Blessed Paul VI closely links joy and *parrhesia*. While lamenting a "lack of joy and hope" as an obstacle to evangelization, he extols the "delightful and comforting joy of evangelizing", linked to "an interior enthusiasm that nobody and nothing can quench". This ensures that the world does not receive the Gospel "from evangelizers who are dejected [and] discouraged". During the 1975 Holy Year, Pope Paul devoted to joy his Apostolic Exhortation *Gaudete in Domino* (9 May 1975): AAS 67 (1975), 289-322.

132. *Parrhesía* is a seal of the Spirit; it testifies to the authenticity of our preaching. It is a joyful assurance that leads us to glory in the Gospel we proclaim. It is an unshakeable trust in the faithful Witness who gives us the certainty that nothing can "separate us from the love of God" (*Rom* 8:39).

133. We need the Spirit's prompting, lest we be paralyzed by fear and excessive caution, lest we grow used to keeping within safe bounds. Let us remember that closed spaces grow musty and unhealthy. When the Apostles were tempted to let themselves be crippled by danger and threats, they joined in prayer to implore *parrhesía*: "And now, Lord, look upon their threats, and grant to your servants to speak your word with all boldness" (*Acts* 4:29). As a result, "when they had prayed, the place in which they were gathered together was shaken; and they were all filled with the Holy Spirit and spoke the word of God with boldness" (*Acts* 4:31).

134. Like the prophet Jonah, we are constantly tempted to flee to a safe haven. It can have many names: individualism, spiritualism, living in a little world, addiction, intransigence, the rejection of new ideas and approaches, dogmatism, nostalgia, pessimism, hiding behind rules and regulations. We can resist having to leave behind a familiar and easy way of doing things. Yet the challenges involved can be like the storm, the whale, the worm that dried the gourd plant, or the wind and sun that burned Jonah's head. For us, as for him, they can serve to bring us back to the God of tenderness, who invites us to set out ever anew on our journey.

135. God is eternal newness. He impels us constantly to set out anew, to pass beyond what is familiar, to the fringes and beyond. He takes us to where humanity is most wounded, where men and women, beneath the appearance of a shallow conformity, continue to seek an answer to the question of life's meaning. God is not afraid! He is fearless! He is always greater than our plans and schemes. Unafraid of the fringes, he himself became a fringe (cf. *Phil* 2:6-8; *Jn* 1:14). So if we dare to go to the fringes, we will find him there; indeed, he is already there. Jesus is already there, in the hearts of our brothers and sisters, in their wounded flesh, in their troubles and in their profound desolation. He is already there.

136. True enough, we need to open the door of our hearts to Jesus, who stands and knocks (cf. *Rev* 3:20). Sometimes I wonder, though, if perhaps Jesus is already inside us and knocking on the door for us to let him escape from our stale self-centeredness. In the Gospel, we see how Jesus "went through the cities and villages, preaching and bringing the good news of the kingdom of God" (*Lk* 8:1). After the resurrection, when the disciples went forth in all directions, the Lord accompanied them (cf. *Mk* 16:20). This is what happens as the result of true encounter.

137. Complacency is seductive; it tells us that there is no point in trying to change things, that there is nothing we can do, because this is the way things have always been and yet we always manage to survive. By force of habit we no longer stand up to evil. We "let things be", or as others have decided they ought to be. Yet let us allow the Lord to rouse us from our torpor, to free us from our inertia. Let us rethink our usual way of doing things; let us open our eyes and ears, and above all our hearts, so as not to be complacent about things as they are, but unsettled by the living and effective word of the risen Lord.

138. We are inspired to act by the example of all those priests, religious, and laity who devote themselves to proclamation and to serving others with great fidelity, often at the risk of their lives and certainly at the cost of their comfort. Their testimony reminds us that, more than bureaucrats and functionaries, the Church needs passionate missionaries, enthusiastic about sharing true life. The saints surprise us, they confound us, because by their lives they urge us to abandon a dull and dreary mediocrity.

139. Let us ask the Lord for the grace not to hesitate when the Spirit calls us to take a step forward. Let us ask for the apostolic courage to share the Gospel with others and to stop trying to make our Christian life a museum of memories. In every situation, may the Holy Spirit cause us to contemplate history in the light of the risen Jesus. In this way, the Church will not stand still, but constantly welcome the Lord's surprises.

In Community

140. When we live apart from others, it is very difficult to fight against concupiscence, the snares and temptations of the devil and the selfishness of the world. Bombarded as we are by so many enticements, we can grow too isolated, lose our sense of reality and inner clarity, and easily succumb.

141. Growth in holiness is a journey in community, side by side with others. We see this in some holy communities. From time to time, the Church has canonized entire communities that lived the Gospel heroically or offered to God the lives of all their members. We can think, for example, of the seven holy founders of the Order of the Servants of Mary, the seven blessed sisters of the first monastery of the Visitation in Madrid, the Japanese martyrs Saint Paul Miki and companions, the Korean martyrs Saint Andrew Taegon and companions, or the South American martyrs Saint Roque González, Saint Alonso Rodríguez and companions. We should also remember the more recent witness borne by the Blessed Trappists of Tibhirine, Algeria, who prepared as a community for martyrdom. In many holy marriages too, each spouse becomes a means used by Christ for the sanctification of the other. Living or working alongside others is surely a path of spiritual growth. Saint John of the Cross told one of his followers: "You are living with others in order to be fashioned and tried".[104]

---

[104] *Precautions*, 15.

142. Each community is called to create a "God-enlightened space in which to experience the hidden presence of the risen Lord".[105] Sharing the word and celebrating the Eucharist together fosters fraternity and makes us a holy and missionary community. It also gives rise to authentic and shared mystical experiences. Such was the case with Saints Benedict and Scholastica. We can also think of the sublime spiritual experience shared by Saint Augustine and his mother, Saint Monica. "As the day now approached on which she was to depart this life, a day known to you but not to us, it came about, as I believe by your secret arrangement, that she and I stood alone leaning in a window that looked onto a garden... We opened wide our hearts to drink in the streams of your fountain, the source of life that is in you... And as we spoke of that wisdom and strained after it, we touched it in some measure by the impetus of our hearts... eternal life might be like that one moment of knowledge which we now sighed after".[106]

143. Such experiences, however, are neither the most frequent nor the most important. The common life, whether in the family, the parish, the religious community or any other, is made up of small everyday things. This was true of the holy community formed by Jesus, Mary and Joseph, which reflected in an exemplary way the beauty of the Trinitarian communion. It

[105] John Paul II, Apostolic Exhortation *Vita Consecrata* (25 March 1996), 42: AAS 88 (1996), 416.
[106] *Confessiones*, IX, 10, 23-25: PL 32, 773-775.

was also true of the life that Jesus shared with his disciples and with ordinary people.

144. Let us not forget that Jesus asked his disciples to pay attention to details.

The little detail that wine was running out at a party.

The little detail that one sheep was missing.

The little detail of noticing the widow who offered her two small coins.

The little detail of having spare oil for the lamps, should the bridegroom delay.

The little detail of asking the disciples how many loaves of bread they had.

The little detail of having a fire burning and a fish cooking as he waited for the disciples at daybreak.

145. A community that cherishes the little details of love,[107] whose members care for one another and create an open and evangelizing environment, is a place where the risen Lord is present, sanctifying it in accordance with the Father's plan. There are times when, by a gift of the Lord's love, we are granted, amid these little details, consoling experiences of God. "One winter night I was carrying out my little duty as usual… Suddenly, I heard off in the distance

---

[107] I think especially of the three key words "please", "thank you" and "sorry". "The right words, spoken at the right time, daily protect and nurture love": Post-Synodal Apostolic Exhortation *Amoris Laetitia* (19 March 2016), 133: AAS 108 (2016), 363.

the harmonious sound of a musical instrument. I then pictured a well-lighted drawing room, brilliantly gilded, filled with elegantly dressed young ladies conversing together and conferring upon each other all sorts of compliments and other worldly remarks. Then my glance fell upon the poor invalid whom I was supporting. Instead of the beautiful strains of music I heard only her occasional complaints… I cannot express in words what happened in my soul; what I know is that the Lord illumined it with rays of truth which so surpassed the dark brilliance of earthly feasts that I could not believe my happiness".[108]

146. Contrary to the growing consumerist individualism that tends to isolate us in a quest for well-being apart from others, our path to holiness can only make us identify all the more with Jesus' prayer "that all may be one; even as you, Father, are in me, and I in you" (*Jn* 17:21).

IN CONSTANT PRAYER

147. Finally, though it may seem obvious, we should remember that holiness consists in a habitual openness to the transcendent, expressed in prayer and adoration. The saints are distinguished by a spirit of prayer and a need for communion with God. They find an exclusive concern with this world to be narrow and stifling, and, amid their own concerns and commitments, they long

[108] Thérèse of the Child Jesus, Manuscript C, 29 v-30r.

for God, losing themselves in praise and contemplation of the Lord. I do not believe in holiness without prayer, even though that prayer need not be lengthy or involve intense emotions.

148. Saint John of the Cross tells us: "Endeavour to remain always in the presence of God, either real, imaginative, or unitive, insofar as is permitted by your works".[109] In the end, our desire for God will surely find expression in our daily lives: "Try to be continuous in prayer, and in the midst of bodily exercises do not leave it. Whether you eat, drink, talk with others, or do anything, always go to God and attach your heart to him".[110]

149. For this to happen, however, some moments spent alone with God are also necessary. For Saint Teresa of Avila, prayer "is nothing but friendly intercourse, and frequent solitary converse, with him who we know loves us".[111] I would insist that this is true not only for a privileged few, but for all of us, for "we all have need of this silence, filled with the presence of him who is adored".[112] Trust-filled prayer is a response of a heart open to encountering God face to face, where all is peaceful and the quiet voice of the Lord can be heard in the midst of silence.

[109] *Degrees of Perfection*, 2.
[110] Id., *Counsels to a Religious on How to Attain Perfection*, 9.
[111] *Autobiography*, 8, 5.
[112] John Paul II, Apostolic Letter *Orientale Lumen* (2 May 1995), 16: AAS 87 (1995), 762.

150. In that silence, we can discern, in the light of the Spirit, the paths of holiness to which the Lord is calling us. Otherwise, any decisions we make may only be window-dressing that, rather than exalting the Gospel in our lives, will mask or submerge it. For each disciple, it is essential to spend time with the Master, to listen to his words, and to learn from him always. Unless we listen, all our words will be nothing but useless chatter.

151. We need to remember that "contemplation of the face of Jesus, died and risen, restores our humanity, even when it has been broken by the troubles of this life or marred by sin. We must not domesticate the power of the face of Christ".[113] So let me ask you: Are there moments when you place yourself quietly in the Lord's presence, when you calmly spend time with him, when you bask in his gaze? Do you let his fire inflame your heart? Unless you let him warm you more and more with his love and tenderness, you will not catch fire. How will you then be able to set the hearts of others on fire by your words and witness? If, gazing on the face of Christ, you feel unable to let yourself be healed and transformed, then enter into the Lord's heart, into his wounds, for that is the abode of divine mercy.[114]

152. I ask that we never regard prayerful silence as a form of escape and rejection of the world around us.

---

[113] *Meeting with the Participants in the Fifth Convention of the Italian Church*, Florence, (10 November 2015): AAS 107 (2015), 1284.

[114] Cf. Bernard of Clairvaux, *Sermones in Canticum Canticorum*, 61, 3-5: PL 183:1071-1073.

The Russian pilgrim, who prayed constantly, says that such prayer did not separate him from what was happening all around him. "Everybody was kind to me; it was as though everyone loved me... Not only did I feel [happiness and consolation] in my own soul, but the whole outside world also seemed to me full of charm and delight".[115]

153. Nor does history vanish. Prayer, because it is nourished by the gift of God present and at work in our lives, must always be marked by remembrance. The memory of God's works is central to the experience of the covenant between God and his people. God wished to enter history, and so our prayer is interwoven with memories. We think back not only on his revealed Word, but also on our own lives, the lives of others, and all that the Lord has done in his Church. This is the grateful memory that Saint Ignatius of Loyola refers to in his *Contemplation for Attaining Love*,[116] when he asks us to be mindful of all the blessings we have received from the Lord. Think of your own history when you pray, and there you will find much mercy. This will also increase your awareness that the Lord is ever mindful of you; he never forgets you. So it makes sense to ask him to shed light on the smallest details of your life, for he sees them all.

154. Prayer of supplication is an expression of a heart that trusts in God and realizes that of itself it can do

---

[115] *The Way of a Pilgrim*, New York, 1965, pp. 17, 105-106.
[116] Cf. *Spiritual Exercises*, 230-237.

nothing. The life of God's faithful people is marked by constant supplication born of faith-filled love and great confidence. Let us not downplay prayer of petition, which so often calms our hearts and helps us persevere in hope. Prayer of intercession has particular value, for it is an act of trust in God and, at the same time, an expression of love for our neighbor. There are those who think, based on a one-sided spirituality, that prayer should be unalloyed contemplation of God, free of all distraction, as if the names and faces of others were somehow an intrusion to be avoided. Yet in reality, our prayer will be all the more pleasing to God and more effective for our growth in holiness if, through intercession, we attempt to practice the twofold commandment that Jesus left us. Intercessory prayer is an expression of our fraternal concern for others, since we are able to embrace their lives, their deepest troubles and their loftiest dreams. Of those who commit themselves generously to intercessory prayer we can apply the words of Scripture: "This is a man who loves the brethren and prays much for the people" (2 Mac 15:14).

155. If we realize that God exists, we cannot help but worship him, at times in quiet wonder, and praise him in festive song. We thus share in the experience of Blessed Charles de Foucauld, who said: "As soon as I believed that there was a God, I understood that I could do nothing other than to live for him".[117] In the life of God's pilgrim people, there can be many simple gestures of pure adoration, as when "the gaze of a

[117] Letter to Henry de Castries, 14 August 1901.

pilgrim rests on an image that symbolizes God's affection and closeness. Love pauses, contemplates the mystery, and enjoys it in silence".[118]

156. The prayerful reading of God's word, which is "sweeter than honey" (*Ps* 119:103) yet a "two-edged sword" (*Heb* 4:12), enables us to pause and listen to the voice of the Master. It becomes a lamp for our steps and a light for our path (cf. *Ps* 119:105). As the bishops of India have reminded us, "devotion to the word of God is not simply one of many devotions, beautiful but somewhat optional. It goes to the very heart and identity of Christian life. The word has the power to transform lives".[119]

157. Meeting Jesus in the Scriptures leads us to the Eucharist, where the written word attains its greatest efficacy, for there the living Word is truly present. In the Eucharist, the one true God receives the greatest worship the world can give him, for it is Christ himself who is offered. When we receive him in Holy Communion, we renew our covenant with him and allow him to carry out ever more fully his work of transforming our lives.

[118] Fifth General Conference of the Latin American and Caribbean Bishops, *Aparecida Document* (29 June 2007), 259.
[119] Conference of Catholic Bishops of India, *Final Declaration of the Twenty-First Plenary Assembly*, 18 February 2009, 3.2.

CHAPTER FIVE

SPIRITUAL COMBAT, VIGILANCE AND DISCERNMENT

158. The Christian life is a constant battle. We need strength and courage to withstand the temptations of the devil and to proclaim the Gospel. This battle is sweet, for it allows us to rejoice each time the Lord triumphs in our lives.

COMBAT AND VIGILANCE

159. We are not dealing merely with a battle against the world and a worldly mentality that would deceive us and leave us dull and mediocre, lacking in enthusiasm and joy. Nor can this battle be reduced to the struggle against our human weaknesses and proclivities (be they laziness, lust, envy, jealousy or any others). It is also a constant struggle against the devil, the prince of evil. Jesus himself celebrates our victories. He rejoiced when his disciples made progress in preaching the Gospel and overcoming the opposition of the evil one: "I saw Satan fall like lightning from heaven" (*Lk* 10:18).

More than a myth

160. We will not admit the existence of the devil if we insist on regarding life by empirical standards alone, without a supernatural understanding. It is precisely the conviction that this malign power is present in our midst that enables us to understand how evil can at times have so much destructive force. True enough, the biblical authors had limited conceptual resources for expressing certain realities, and in Jesus' time epilepsy, for example, could easily be confused with demonic possession. Yet this should not lead us to an oversimplification that would conclude that all the cases related in the Gospel had to do with psychological disorders and hence that the devil does not exist or is not at work. He is present in the very first pages of the Scriptures, which end with God's victory over the devil.[120] Indeed, in leaving us the Our Father, Jesus wanted us to conclude by asking the Father to "deliver us from evil". That final word does not refer to evil in the abstract; a more exact translation would be "the evil one". It indicates a personal being who assails us. Jesus taught us to ask daily for deliverance from him, lest his power prevail over us.

161. Hence, we should not think of the devil as a myth, a representation, a symbol, a figure of speech or

---

[120] Cf. Homily at Mass in Casa Santa Marta, 11 October 2013: *L'Osservatore Romano*, 12 October 2013, p. 2.

an idea.[121] This mistake would lead us to let down our guard, to grow careless and end up more vulnerable. The devil does not need to possess us. He poisons us with the venom of hatred, desolation, envy and vice. When we let down our guard, he takes advantage of it to destroy our lives, our families and our communities. "Like a roaring lion, he prowls around, looking for someone to devour" (*1 Pet* 5:8).

Alert and trustful

162. God's word invites us clearly to "stand against the wiles of the devil" (*Eph* 6:11) and to "quench all the flaming darts of the evil one" (*Eph* 6:16). These expressions are not melodramatic, precisely because our path towards holiness is a constant battle. Those who do not realize this will be prey to failure or mediocrity. For this spiritual combat, we can count on the powerful weapons that the Lord has given us: faith-filled prayer, meditation on the word of God, the celebration of Mass, Eucharistic adoration, sacramental Reconciliation, works of charity, community life, missionary outreach. If we become careless, the false

① Rosary & Marian devotion

[121] Cf. Paul VI, *Catechesis*, General Audience of 15 November 1972: *Insegnamenti* X (1972), pp. 1168-1170: "One of our greatest needs is defense against that evil which we call the devil... Evil is not simply a deficiency, it is an efficiency, a living spiritual being, perverted and perverting. A terrible reality, mysterious and frightful. They no longer remain within the framework of biblical and ecclesiastical teaching who refuse to recognize its existence, or who make of it an independent principle that does not have, like every creature, its origin in God, or explain it as a pseudo-reality, a conceptual and imaginative personification of the hidden causes of our misfortunes".

promises of evil will easily seduce us. As the sainted Cura Brochero observed: "What good is it when Lucifer promises you freedom and showers you with all his benefits, if those benefits are false, deceptive and poisonous?"[122]

163. Along this journey, the cultivation of all that is good, progress in the spiritual life and growth in love are the best counterbalance to evil. Those who choose to remain neutral, who are satisfied with little, who renounce the ideal of giving themselves generously to the Lord, will never hold out. Even less if they fall into defeatism, for "if we start without confidence, we have already lost half the battle and we bury our talents… Christian triumph is always a cross, yet a cross which is at the same time a victorious banner, borne with aggressive tenderness against the assaults of evil".[123]

Spiritual corruption

164. The path of holiness is a source of peace and joy, given to us by the Spirit. At the same time, it demands that we keep "our lamps lit" (Lk 12:35) and be attentive. "Abstain from every form of evil" (*1 Thess* 5:22). "Keep awake" (Mt 24:42; Mk 13:35). "Let us not fall asleep" (*1 Thess* 5:6). Those who think they commit no grievous sins against God's law can fall into a state

[122] José Gabriel del Rosario Brochero, "Plática de las banderas", in Conferencia Episcopal Argentina, *El Cura Brochero. Cartas y sermones*, Buenos Aires, 1999, 71.
[123] Apostolic Exhortation *Evangelii Gaudium* (24 November 2013), 85: AAS 105 (2013), 1056.

of dull lethargy. Since they see nothing serious to reproach themselves with, they fail to realize that their spiritual life has gradually turned lukewarm. They end up weakened and corrupted.

165. Spiritual corruption is worse than the fall of a sinner, for it is a comfortable and self-satisfied form of blindness. Everything then appears acceptable: deception, slander, egotism and other subtle forms of self-centeredness, for "even Satan disguises himself as an angel of light" (*2 Cor* 11:14). So Solomon ended his days, whereas David, who sinned greatly, was able to make up for disgrace. Jesus warned us against this self-deception that easily leads to corruption. He spoke of a person freed from the devil who, convinced that his life was now in order, ended up being possessed by seven other evil spirits (cf. *Lk* 11:24-26). Another biblical text puts it bluntly: "The dog turns back to his own vomit" (*2 Pet* 2:22; cf. *Pr* 26:11).

Discernment

166. How can we know if something comes from the Holy Spirit or if it stems from the spirit of the world or the spirit of the devil? The only way is through discernment, which calls for something more than intelligence or common sense. It is a gift which we must implore. If we ask with confidence that the Holy Spirit grant us this gift, and then seek to develop it through prayer, reflection, reading and good counsel, then surely we will grow in this spiritual endowment.

An urgent need

167. The gift of discernment has become all the more necessary today, since contemporary life offers immense possibilities for action and distraction, and the world presents all of them as valid and good. All of us, but especially the young, are immersed in a culture of zapping. We can navigate simultaneously on two or more screens and interact at the same time with two or three virtual scenarios. Without the wisdom of discernment, we can easily become prey to every passing trend.

168. This is all the more important when some novelty presents itself in our lives. Then we have to decide whether it is new wine brought by God or an illusion created by the spirit of this world or the spirit of the devil. At other times, the opposite can happen, when the forces of evil induce us not to change, to leave things as they are, to opt for a rigid resistance to change. Yet that would be to block the working of the Spirit. We are free, with the freedom of Christ. Still, he asks us to examine what is within us – our desires, anxieties, fears and questions – and what takes place all around us – "the signs of the times" – and thus to recognize the paths that lead to complete freedom. "Test everything; hold fast to what is good" (*1 Thess* 5:21).

Always in the light of the Lord

169. Discernment is necessary not only at extraordinary times, when we need to resolve grave problems and make crucial decisions. It is a means of spiritual combat for helping us to follow the Lord more faithfully. We need it at all times, to help us recognize God's timetable, lest we fail to heed the promptings of his grace and disregard his invitation to grow. Often discernment is exercised in small and apparently irrelevant things, since greatness of spirit is manifested in simple everyday realities.[124] It involves striving untrammeled for all that is great, better and more beautiful, while at the same time being concerned for the little things, for each day's responsibilities and commitments. For this reason, I ask all Christians not to omit, in dialogue with the Lord, a sincere daily "examination of conscience". Discernment also enables us to recognize the concrete means that the Lord provides in his mysterious and loving plan, to make us move beyond mere good intentions.

A supernatural gift   *where do we look?*

170. Certainly, spiritual discernment does not exclude existential, psychological, sociological or moral insights drawn from the human sciences. At the same time, it transcends them. Nor are the Church's sound norms sufficient. We should always remember that discernment is a grace. Even though it includes reason and prudence, it goes beyond them, for it seeks a glimpse of that unique and mysterious plan that God has for each of us, which takes shape amid so many varied

---

[124] The tomb of Saint Ignatius of Loyola bears this thought-provoking inscription: *Non coerceri a maximo, contineri tamen a minimo divinum est* ("Not to be confined by the greatest, yet to be contained within the smallest, is truly divine").

situations and limitations. It involves more than my temporal well-being, my satisfaction at having accomplished something useful, or even my desire for peace of mind. It has to do with the meaning of my life before the Father who knows and loves me, with the real purpose of my life, that nobody knows better than he. Ultimately, discernment leads to the wellspring of undying life: to know the Father, the only true God, and the one whom he has sent, Jesus Christ (cf. *Jn* 17:3). It requires no special abilities, nor is it only for the more intelligent or better educated. The Father readily reveals himself to the lowly (cf. *Mt* 11:25).

171. The Lord speaks to us in a variety of ways, at work, through others and at every moment. Yet we simply cannot do without the silence of prolonged prayer, which enables us better to perceive God's language, to interpret the real meaning of the inspirations we believe we have received, to calm our anxieties and to see the whole of our existence afresh in his own light. In this way, we allow the birth of a new synthesis that springs from a life inspired by the Spirit.

Speak, Lord

172. Nonetheless, it is possible that, even in prayer itself, we could refuse to let ourselves be confronted by the freedom of the Spirit, who acts as he wills. We must remember that prayerful discernment must be born of a readiness to listen: to the Lord and to others, and to reality itself, which always challenges us in new ways. Only if we are prepared to listen, do we have the

freedom to set aside our own partial or insufficient ideas, our usual habits and ways of seeing things. In this way, we become truly open to accepting a call that can shatter our security, but lead us to a better life. It is not enough that everything be calm and peaceful. God may be offering us something more, but in our comfortable inadvertence, we do not recognize it.

173. Naturally, this attitude of listening entails obedience to the Gospel as the ultimate standard, but also to the Magisterium that guards it, as we seek to find in the treasury of the Church whatever is most fruitful for the "today" of salvation. It is not a matter of applying rules or repeating what was done in the past, since the same solutions are not valid in all circumstances and what was useful in one context may not prove so in another. The discernment of spirits liberates us from rigidity, which has no place before the perennial "today" of the risen Lord. The Spirit alone can penetrate what is obscure and hidden in every situation, and grasp its every nuance, so that the newness of the Gospel can emerge in another light.

The logic of the gift and of the cross

174. An essential condition for progress in discernment is a growing understanding of God's patience and his timetable, which are never our own. God does not pour down fire upon those who are unfaithful (cf. *Lk* 9:54), or allow the zealous to uproot the tares growing among the wheat (cf. *Mt* 13:29). Generosity too is demanded, for "it is more blessed to give than to receive" (*Acts* 20:35). Discernment is not about discovering what more we can get out of this life, but about recognizing how we can better accomplish the mission entrusted to us at our baptism. This entails a readiness to make sacrifices, even to sacrificing everything. For happiness is a paradox. We experience it most when we accept the mysterious logic that is not of this world: "This is our logic", says Saint Bonaventure,[125] pointing to the cross. Once we enter into this dynamic, we will not let our consciences be numbed and we will open ourselves generously to discernment.

175. When, in God's presence, we examine our life's journey, no areas can be off limits. In all aspects of life we can continue to grow and offer something greater to God, even in those areas we find most difficult. We need, though, to ask the Holy Spirit to liberate us and to expel the fear that makes us ban him from certain parts of our lives. God asks everything of us, yet he also gives everything to us. He does not want to enter our lives to cripple or diminish them, but to bring them to fulfilment. Discernment, then, is not a solipsistic self-analysis or a form of egotistical introspection, but an authentic process of leaving ourselves behind in order to approach the mystery of God, who helps us to carry out the mission to which he has called us, for the good of our brothers and sisters.

---

[125] *Collationes in Hexaemeron*, 1, 30.

176. I would like these reflections to be crowned by Mary, because she lived the Beatitudes of Jesus as none other. She is that woman who rejoiced in the presence of God, who treasured everything in her heart, and who let herself be pierced by the sword. Mary is the saint among the saints, blessed above all others. She teaches us the way of holiness and she walks ever at our side. She does not let us remain fallen and at times she takes us into her arms without judging us. Our converse with her consoles, frees and sanctifies us. Mary our Mother does not need a flood of words. She does not need us to tell her what is happening in our lives. All we need do is whisper, time and time again: "Hail Mary…"

177. It is my hope that these pages will prove helpful by enabling the whole Church to devote herself anew to promoting the desire for holiness. Let us ask the Holy Spirit to pour out upon us a fervent longing to be saints for God's greater glory, and let us encourage one another in this effort. In this way, we will share a happiness that the world will not be able to take from us.

Given in Rome, at Saint Peter's, on 19 March, the Solemnity of Saint Joseph, in the year 2018, the sixth of my Pontificate.

CHAPTER SUMMARIES AND DISCUSSION QUESTIONS

Mark-David Janus, CSP, PhD

REJOICE AND BE GLAD: INTRODUCTION

SUMMARY: Pope Francis is offering reflections on practical holiness. This is not a comprehensive theological reflection on holiness, but an appeal to all people, especially those "persecuted or humiliated" to remember that the Lord is calling them to be saints.

1. How practical is holiness?

2. When Pope Francis says God wants us to be saints, what do you hear?

CHAPTER ONE: THE CALL TO HOLINESS

THE SAINTS WHO ENCOURAGE AND ACCOMPANY US

SUMMARY: The Holy Father begins by calling to mind the communion of saints, those canonized as well as those whose sanctity is known privately, even the members of our families. Because no one is saved alone, but only as part of a community, God sends saints into our lives to help us. The saints, living and dead, are on our side. The Pope disabuses us of the notion that saints are perfect people—he sees saints as people on a journey toward God.

1. What is a saint?

2. Do you have favorite saints? Who and why?

3. Pope Francis includes in the Communion of Saints people who may be our family members; who in your life would you call a saint?

4. The Holy Father writes of the saints, "Their lives may not always have been perfect, yet even amid their faults and failings they kept moving forward and proved pleasing to the Lord." Can you see yourself in this definition?

THE SAINTS "NEXT DOOR"

SUMMARY: The people of God together are called to be holy. No one is saved alone, but as part of a vast network of relationships. Within this network of human relationships are people of great patience and perseverance, parents, friends, neighbors, husbands and wives, all who reflect to us God's presence. Unknown to history, these everyday saints are the "middle class of holiness." Many of these saints do not belong to the Roman Catholic Church.

1. Increasingly, people describe themselves as spiritual but not religious. Pope Francis says, "No one is saved alone," and that "we are never completely

ourselves unless we belong to a people." What role does belonging play in your spiritual life?

2. Patience is described as a quality of everyday sanctity; how has someone's patience benefited your life?

3. The Holy Father speculates that only at our death will we really be able to appreciate all those people who contributed to important moments in our personal life. Can you recall an experience of discovering, much later, someone who benefited your life even though you did not know it at the time?

4. Who is your favorite saint outside the Roman Catholic Church?

THE LORD CALLS

SUMMARY: The call to holiness comes from God, and the examples of all the saints who have gone before us are to encourage, not discourage us. We don't copy the lives of the saints, but we are inspired by them to search out our unique form of holiness, for "God's life is communicated 'to some in one way and to others in another.'" There is also a special papal shout-out to women who are saints, both the famous as well as those unknown.

1. Why do you think you are not good enough to be a saint?

2. The Pope writes, "The important thing is that each believer discerns his or her own path, that they bring out the very best of themselves,

the most personal gifts God has placed in their hearts." How do you go about doing that?

3. Pope Francis highlights the special gifts of the women saints. From among the canonized saints, or the personal saints in your life, name at least one saintly woman who has inspired you.

FOR YOU TOO

SUMMARY: Holiness belongs to everyone and is found in the life you are living every day. Holiness is something we grow toward and into. The Church, composed of sinners, the Pope is quick to remind us, is there to help us with Scripture, sacrament, and witness of people's lives. Small gestures of love and kindness help us grow in holiness step by step.

1. "We are all called to be holy by living our lives with love": how does that work out for you?

2. What in the Church and the traditions of the Church do you find helpful in your search for holiness?

3. The Pope speaks about taking small, daily, practical steps toward holiness. If you looked back on a week, can you see yourself taking some of those steps?

YOUR MISSION IN CHRIST

SUMMARY: Pope Francis encourages all of us to "see the entirety of your life as a mission." Our mission is unique to our time and place. We discover it by reflecting on the life of Jesus and by seeking the guidance of the Holy Spirit. Like the saints that have gone before us, we are not always clear about what our mission is, nor do we carry it out without mistakes. Slowly we grow in understanding and carrying out our mission, "the message of Jesus that God wants to speak to the world by your life."

1. Pope Francis says, "Each saint is a mission" and "Every saint is a message." What is your mission, and what would you like your message to be?

2. "Not everything a saint says is completely faithful to the Gospel; not everything he or she does is authentic or perfect." In your journey to holiness, how do you keep yourself from focusing on your mistakes and keep your eye on your mission?

ACTIVITY THAT SANCTIFIES

SUMMARY: This section can be summarized with the words, "Life does not have a mission, but is a mission." The mission is to identify with Christ in building the kingdom of God; consequently our mission is not to withdraw from the world but embrace it—for everything in the world can be part of our pathway to holiness. Because the world is often "a rat race," we need moments of solitude with God. "Sooner or later," the Pope says, "we have to face our true selves and let the Lord enter." It is here we discover the motivation and commitment for our work. Solitude and service are needed for holiness.

1. "Your identification with Christ and his will involves a commitment to build with him that kingdom of love, justice and universal peace." How do you find yourself building the kingdom of God with Christ?

2. For the Pope, action must be balanced with prayer: "Sooner or later, we have to face our true selves and let the Lord enter." How does daily life interfere with you finding time for that kind of encounter with the Lord?

MORE ALIVE, MORE HUMAN

SUMMARY: Pope Francis reassures us that our call to holiness is a call to get more, not less, out of life. Even those faced with great suffering, can find peace in their journey toward holiness. To be a saint is "to allow yourself to be loved and liberated by God" and guided by the Holy Spirit.

1. To be a saint is "to allow yourself to be loved and liberated by God"; has that happened for you? What gets in the way?

2. The Pope mentions the Holy Spirit a lot. When you think of the Holy Spirit, what do you think of?

3. True or false for you: "The only great tragedy in life, is not to become a saint."

CHAPTER TWO: TWO SUBTLE ENEMIES OF HOLINESS

SUMMARY: Holiness has enemies, and Pope Francis focuses attention on two traditional theological errors that he sees sneaking their way into contemporary religion. Gnosticism is a strict and "pure" religious attitude that favors absolute theological certainty over the struggles of real life experience. Pelagianism is religious perfectionism that does not admit human weakness. Pope Francis finds answer to these errors in the doctrine of justification, namely that all human beings are saved by God's grace, not our works, not by our merits but by God's mercy.

1. Pope Francis is going to spend a long time talking about enemies of holiness; before we get his thoughts, what would you say are the enemies of holiness?

CONTEMPORARY GNOSTICISM

An intellect without God and without flesh

Pope Francis has two objections to the religious attitude he identifies as contemporary gnosticism. First, he sees it as primarily an intellectual conception of God developed apart from the real and messy experience of human beings. Second, these gnostic Christians "absolutize their own theories and force others to submit to their way of thinking." Pope Francis believes God is a God of surprises before whose action we need to be humbly attentive.

1. Pope Francis is quite critical of people who judge others based on their ability to understand complex doctrines. Do you think there are elements of the Church that have become overly concerned about doctrine? In what way is doctrine important?

2. "Gnostics think that their explanations can make the entirety of the faith and the Gospel perfectly comprehensible. They...force others to submit to their way of thinking." Why do you think religious people try to force others to submit to their way of thinking? Have you ever noticed this impulse in yourself?

3. The Pope observes that there is something attractive about a strict, pure, orderly religion that explains everything in life. What's wrong with that?

A doctrine without mystery

SUMMARY: In their creation of clear theology of God, gnostics miss the experience of God, limiting what God can do and where God can be. Gnostics are false prophets who in pursuit of clarity and control cannot see the God of surprises who comes to human beings on his own terms.

1. The Holy Father writes, "Even when someone's life appears completely wrecked, even when we see it devastated by vices or addictions, God is present there." What do you think?

2. God "is full of surprises," the Pope writes. How does God surprise you?

The limits of reason

SUMMARY: Pope Francis believes "it is not easy to grasp the truth we have received from the Lord." Consequently, within the Church there are different and legitimate ways of interpreting doctrine and applying it to Christian life. He understands that "for those who long for a monolithic body of doctrine guarded by all and leaving no room for nuance, this might appear as undesirable and leading to confusion," but the incarnation of Jesus leaves us no choice but to be humble before the mercy of God.

1. "There legitimately coexist different ways of interpreting many aspects of doctrine and Christian life." How do you think most Catholics would respond to this statement from the Pope?

2. Do you think Pope Francis is opening the door to confusion, and is that a good or a bad thing for the Church?

3. St. John Paull II warned that people who know a lot about Church doctrine can easily think they are superior to other Christians. What do you think people who don't know a lot about theology have to teach the Church?

CONTEMPORARY PELAGIANISM

SUMMARY: If gnostics fell in love with their intellectual construction of the faith, pelagians are in love with the power of the human will, not the mercy of God.

A will lacking humility

SUMMARY: Contemporary pelagians overestimate human ability. In their zeal they are unaware and intolerant of human weakness. It is only when people are aware of their own weaknesses that God's grace has its way with us. Grace transforms us only gradually, and only when we become aware of God's love in such a way, "that we dwell in him....He is our temple....In him is our holiness."

1. The Pope is critical of believers who "ultimately trust only in their own powers and feel superior to others because they observe certain rules or remain intransigently faithful to a particular Catholic style." How big a problem is this?

2. Some Catholics think that to be a saint they must be perfect and are very critical of themselves when they are not, but Pope Francis says that only when we recognize our limitations, accepting that "we can't do everything" that grace works in us. What is your experience?

3. Pope Francis teaches that grace does not make us superhuman all at once. Grace acts in history and transforms us gradually. Do you find this encouraging? If so, why?

An often overlooked Church teaching

SUMMARY: Pope Francis reminds us of the doctrine of justification: "we are justified not by our own works or efforts, but by the grace of the Lord, who always takes the initiative." For Pope Francis, God always reaches out to us first. We respond to God's love in recognizing that our life is his gift, and our freedom, his grace.

1. Pope Francis teaches that God always takes the first step: God offers us mercy and then we grow. It is not what we do for God, it is what God does for us. How does this influence your relationship with God?

2. "We must first belong to God, offering ourselves to him who was there first, and entrusting to him our abilities, our efforts, our struggle against evil and our creativity, so that his free gift may grow and develop within us." Do you "belong to God" in this way?

New pelagians

SUMMARY: Pope Francis has harsh words for those whose religious understanding is based on their own will, efforts, and abilities. This attitude makes people self-centered, self-absorbed, punctilious, and elitist. This attitude makes the Church a "museum piece" obsessed with ecclesial rules and structures, bereft of the joy of the Gospel.

1. Pope Francis encourages Christians to set aside their own preoccupations and let themselves be led by the Spirit, passionate about communicating the joy of the Gospel and passionate about seeking out the lost that thirst for Christ. What needs to change in our lives for this to happen?

2. The Pope is critical when he says, "Not infrequently, contrary to the promptings of the Spirit, the life of the Church can become a museum piece or the possession of a select few. This can occur when some groups of Christians give excessive importance to certain rules, customs or ways of acting." Is this something that can be changed, and how can it be done?

3. No one walks around saying they are a modern pelagian, but is it possible, without our noticing it, that we develop religious attitudes and practices that leave "few openings for the working of grace" in our lives, or the lives of others?

The summation of the Law

SUMMARY: Pope Francis finds the antidote to pelagianism in the theological virtues: faith, hope, and love. While pelagians offer a thicket of precepts and prescriptions, the Holy Father teaches, "Jesus clears a way to seeing two faces, that of the Father and that of our brother...or better yet, one alone: the face of God reflected in so many other faces." Rather than pick out our favorite examples of gnostics or pelagians, Pope Francis asks that we examine our lives to see if elements of either of these distortions have worked their way into our lives.

1. In a very powerful image, the Holy Father says Jesus presents us with two faces, that of the Father and that of our fellow human being. Better yet, Jesus gives us only one face, "the face of God reflected

in so many other faces." What makes this difficult for us to grasp, especially with "the least, the most vulnerable, the defenseless and those in need?"

CHAPTER THREE: IN THE LIGHT OF THE MASTER

SUMMARY: Of the many ways one can describe holiness and how to live a holy life, Pope Francis chooses the Sermon on the Mount. He believes the Beatitudes preached by Jesus paint a portrait of Jesus that we can imitate in our lives.

GOING AGAINST THE FLOW

SUMMARY: The Beatitudes have such a poetic air about them we can almost fail to hear their challenge to the way things work in the world. Reading the Beatitudes together with Pope Francis, we ask ourselves how they can change our lives.

"Blessed are the poor in spirit, for theirs is the kingdom of heaven"

1. What role does money, or the search for money play in your life?

2. "Once we think we are rich, we can become so self-satisfied that we leave no room for God's word, for the love of our brothers and sisters, or for the enjoyment of the most important things in life." If we do not make enough room for these things in our lives, what gets in our way?

"Blessed are the meek, for they will inherit the earth"

1. Meekness is not a popular virtue. The Pope sees meekness as the opposite of the pride, which leads someone to think they have a right to dominate others because they are better than others. In the competitive world in which we live, how do we promote meekness as a virtue?

2. Pope Francis also sees meekness as the opposite of the tendency to criticize other people. He quotes Saint Therese, who said, "Perfect charity consists in putting up with other's mistakes, and not being scandalized by their faults." How can we resist the temptation to criticize?

"Blessed are those who mourn, for they will be comforted"

1. Pope Francis understands this Beatitude as the willingness to not ignore the sickness, sorrow, and suffering that surround us. How do we keep from turning our heads away from all those who suffer?

2. The Holy Father suggests that people who imitate the compassion of Jesus are blessed: "They discover the meaning of life by coming to the aid of those who suffer, understanding their anguish and bringing relief." Have you had this experience in your life?

"Blessed are those who hunger and thirst for righteousness, for they will be filled"

1. Pope Francis places this Beatitude against the corruption present in governments and business. In the face of injustice, the temptation is give up the fight, or join the unjust side. Holiness is found when people do not surrender their passion for justice, no matter how long the odds. How do you maintain your passion for justice when you feel worn down?

2. True justice comes about in people's lives when they themselves are just in their decisions, especially when expressed in their pursuit of justice for the poor and the weak. What helps you be just?

"Blessed are the merciful, for they will receive mercy"

1. Mercy has two aspects. It involves giving, helping, and serving others, but it also includes forgiveness and understanding. Which do you find harder to live?

2. The Holy Father reminds us that our practice of mercy will be the yardstick God uses to measure us. Does this make you feel anxious or relieved?

"Blessed are the pure in heart, for they will see God"

1. Pope Francis defines purity of heart as the integrity and passion of our heart, the expression of our deepest desires. A pure heart capable of love "admits nothing that might harm, weaken or endanger that love." How do you purify your heart and keep it pure?

"Blessed are the peacemakers, for they will be called children of God"

1. The Holy Father begins by saying that we cannot ignore the constant wars throughout the world. He asks us to look within and identify whatever is in us creates conflict and division. What instincts lead you to "wage war?"

2. "Sowing peace all around us: that is holiness," Pope Francis says. In your everyday world, how is it that you sow peace?

"Blessed are those who are persecuted for righteousness' sake, for theirs is the kingdom of heaven"

1. Jesus warns that his followers will suffer persecution. Are you aware of the Christians who are suffering persecution, even martyrdom around the world?

2. The Pope warns that people are persecuted because they stand for good and struggle for justice. He suggests any attempt to live the Beatitudes will be viewed negatively, regarded with suspicion, and met with ridicule. Do you know someone who has experienced consequences for the way they have tried to live the Beatitudes? Have you experienced consequences for living your faith?

THE GREAT CRITERION

SUMMARY: Pope Francis reminds us that holiness is judged by the great criterion of Matthew 25: "I was hungry and you gave me food, I was thirsty and you gave me drink, I was a stranger and you welcomed me, I was naked and you clothed me, I was sick and you took care of me, I was in prison and you visited me" (Matt 25:35–36)

In fidelity to the Master

SUMMARY: For Pope Francis, holiness has less to do with ecstasy and more to do with charity—specifically the mystery of seeing Christ in the poor and suffering. The Holy Father tells us that it is his duty to remind us that we simply cannot be a follower of Jesus without actively living mercy for the poor and suffering. This mercy involves individual acts of charity as well as confronting unjust social and economic systems.

1. "Holiness, then, is not about swooning in mystic rapture....We must learn to see him especially in the faces of those with whom he himself wished to be identified...in the poor and the suffering." Have you been able to look at the poor and see the face of Jesus?

2. Pope Francis says it is his duty to warn us that care for the poor and suffering is an essential part of what it means to be a Christian. Is it an essential part of your faith? Of your daily life?

3. Care for the poor also means "the restoration of just social and economic systems." Have you ever had an opportunity to learn about the social teachings of the Church?

SUMMARY: There is an intimate connection between a Christian's personal relationship with the Lord and their "passionate and effective commitment to their neighbors." One cannot be sacrificed for the other. Nor can Christians focus on one issue of concern to the exclusion of the full range of those who suffer. Holiness cannot ignore the demands of social justice. Pope Francis raises the current situations of migrants. He asks that Christians not only stand in the shoes of the migrants, but recognize Jesus in their faces, and remember that this is a demand dating back to the earliest days of the Old Testament.

1. The great saints keep mental prayer, the love of God, and the reading of the Gospel in balance with their passionate and effective commitment to their neighbors. One feeds the other. How do you maintain this vital balance?

2. The Holy Father rejects a Christianity that has no time to be engaged in the social needs of others. He is equally critical of those who confine their concerns to just one social or ethical issue to the neglect of others. How do you think Christians reading this section are going to react to this section of the Pope's letter?

3. The issue of migration is one of the most controversial issues around the world. Pope Francis walks right into the firestorm, saying that for the Christian, "the only proper attitude is to stand in the shoes of those brothers and sisters of ours

who risk their lives to offer a future to their children. Can we not realize that this is exactly what Jesus demands of us, when he tells us that in welcoming the stranger we welcome him (cf. *Mt* 25:35)?" Do you think Catholics will listen to the Pope? Why or why not?

The worship most acceptable to God

SUMMARY: There is an intrinsic link between our worship of God and our active concern for our brothers and sisters. The authenticity of our prayer is measured by our conversion to mercy. There is much in modern life that distracts us from or makes us indifferent to the suffering of others. Reflecting on the Beatitudes and the examples of the great saints help us live the Gospel.

1. "We cannot forget that the ultimate criterion on which our lives will be judged is what we have done for others." Do you think this is how Christians are known around the world? Why or why not?

2. "Our worship becomes pleasing to God when we devote ourselves to living generously, and allow God's gift, granted in prayer, to be shown in our concern for our brothers and sisters." How do you deepen the connection between your private and public prayer and your service of others?

3. The Pope is concerned that the demands of a consumer society and the pace of instant and often superficial social media make it increasingly

difficult for Christians to find the time they need for reflective prayer, and dull their reaction to human suffering. How do you avoid this?

Chapter Four: Signs of Holiness in Today's World

SUMMARY: The challenges of the current time lead Pope Francis to present five aspects of holiness for our attention. These expressions of holiness are in addition to the traditional means of sanctification that are part of the Catholic tradition.

Perseverance, Patience and Meekness

SUMMARY: Perseverance is grounded in the love of God that sustains us. It enables us to deal with the ups and downs of everyday life, as well as to endure hostility, betrayal, and the failing of others. Patience enables us to accompany others no matter how often they fail. Meekness grows from recognizing our own aggressive and selfish inclinations, including the verbal violence so often seen in the media. Meekness is not weakness, it is a love strong enough to place others before ourselves, as well as the strength to demand justice and defend the weak, even when we will suffer for it.

1. Pope Francis relates perseverance with fidelity, the inner strength needed to be faithful to God. This is the same inner strength we need to be faithful to others in good times and in bad. Where does your perseverance come from, and how is it tested?

2. The Holy Father connects the virtue of patience with combatting our internal aggressive and selfish inclinations. He specifically mentions "networks of verbal violence through the internet and the various forums of digital communication." What tests your patience, and how do you stay patient when the victim of verbal violence?

3. When Pope Francis speaks about meekness, he is not speaking about a temperament. He is speaking about an innate respect for other people, "those who keep silent to save their families, who prefer to praise others rather than boast about themselves, or who choose the less welcome tasks, at times even choosing to bear an injustice so as to offer it to the Lord." In a society that does not value meekness, how do you develop a culture of meekness within your soul?

JOY AND A SENSE OF HUMOR

SUMMARY: Joy is a byproduct of a holiness rooted in the knowledge that we are infinitely loved by God. The legacy of the great saints teaches that Christian joy is often accompanied by humor, laughter, and the ability to delight in life. It is a joy not based on the fulfillment of our own needs, but on our communion with God and others.

1. Christian joy is born of the "personal certainty that, when everything is said and done, we are infinitely loved." How do you experience that love?

2. Christian joy is usually accompanied by a sense of humor and an appreciation for the simple beauty of the world. Would you describe your Christianity as humorous and grateful?

3. The Holy Father says joy is "lived in communion, which shares and is shared, since "there is more happiness in giving than in receiving... Fraternal joy increases our capacity for joy, since it makes us capable for rejoicing in the good of others." Does that ring true for you? Are there relationships that increase your capacity for joy? Whose happiness is more important to you than your own?

BOLDNESS AND PASSION

SUMMARY: Like Jesus, Christian holiness is not hesitant, timid, or self-conscious. Boldness and apostolic courage are an essential part of mission. The Holy Spirit inspires us to move beyond what is safe and familiar to the place where "humanity is most wounded...to seek an answer to the question of life's meaning." Christian life is not a "museum of memories" but the gathering of passionate missionaries, enthusiastic about sharing the risen life of Christ.

1. In what ways is your holiness bold and passionate?

2. In your life as a Christian, how do you want to leave your mark in the world?

3. Pope Francis warns us not to be fearful, complacent, afraid of change. He urges us to ask the

Holy Spirit for apostolic courage. Where do you most need courage in your life?

In community

SUMMARY: Holiness is a journey made in community, all sorts of communities: marriages, families, friendships, eucharistic communities, parishes, religious orders. Living or working alongside others is the path to spiritual growth. It is a path consisting of small everyday things, the details of love through which the members of the community care for each other.

1. The Pope believes that "growth in holiness is a journey in community, side by side with others." What communities, relationships, nourish your holiness?

2. "Sharing the word and celebrating the Eucharist together fosters fraternity and makes us a holy and missionary community." Are you part of a community with whom you study the Scripture and celebrate the Eucharist? How does it help you?

3. Communities and relationships that nourish holiness are characterized by "little details of love" that make it possible for people to care for one another and experience the presence of the risen Lord. What details are you good at? What details need your attention? What details are most important to you?

SUMMARY: Prayer is essential to growth in holiness. "For each disciple, it is essential to spend time with the Master, to listen to his words, and to learn from him always." For Pope Francis, prayer is as much listening as speaking. In prayer we allow God to enter our history, into our heart. Through intercessory prayer we show concern for others' needs, and when we pray for ourselves we practice trust in God. The Holy Father notes that devotion to the word of God in the Scriptures and the celebration of the Eucharist has a special place of privilege.

1. Pope Francis says, "I do not believe in holiness without prayer, even though that prayer need not be lengthy or involve intense emotions." Are you able to find time for prayer? How does life conspire to keep you from praying?

2. The Holy Father encourages a type of prayer without words where we gaze on the Lord and we allow the Lord to gaze on us in love. During this time we listen rather than talk. Have you ever tried this style of wordless prayer?

3. The Holy Father also encourages the prayers of petition with which we are most familiar. These prayers are an expression of trust in God and an expression of our concern for our neighbors. How do you go about praying for other people?

4. "Devotion to the word of God is not simply one of many devotions, beautiful but somewhat

optional. It goes to the very heart and identity of Christian life. The word has the power to transform lives." How has reading the Bible gone for you?

5. "In Holy Communion, we…allow him to carry out ever more fully his work of transforming our lives." Why is Holy Communion important to you?

CHAPTER FIVE: SPIRITUAL COMBAT, VIGILANCE AND DISCERNMENT

COMBAT AND VIGILANCE

SUMMARY: Growth in holiness is hindered by forces external to us and by our own weakness. Over and above these obstacles, Pope Francis draws our attention to forces of evil that are arrayed against us: against these we must especially be vigilant. "The devil does not need to possess us. He poisons us with the venom of hatred, desolation, envy and vice."

More than a myth

SUMMARY: The reality of the devil is in the first pages of Scripture and in the life of Jesus, who taught us to pray: "Deliver us from evil." To underestimate the power of evil is a spiritual error.

1. The Pope believes Christians are engaged in a battle, not just with worldly values, and not just with our own human weaknesses, but "against the devil, the prince of evil…a personal being who assails us." Do you believe in evil as a power?

2. When you pray the Lord's prayer, you pray, "Deliver us from evil and lead us not into temptation." What do you mean when you pray this?

3. "The devil does not need to possess us. He poisons us with the venom of hatred, desolation, envy and vice." Have you ever felt evil poisoning you?

Alert and trustful

SUMMARY: Pope Francis identifies carelessness and mediocrity in the spiritual as the most common tools encouraged by the devil. To combat this is the disciplined use of prayer, sacraments, the promotion of the good, and growth in love.

1. Pope Francis believes that carelessness is spiritual danger, as is underestimating the seductive promises of evil. How do you think this happens?

Spiritual corruption

SUMMARY: Pope Francis frequently speaks against corruption in government and business; here he speaks against spiritual corruption, which he identifies as spiritual blindness. This is the lukewarm disciple, without passion, comfortable and self-satisfied, unwilling to see their own sin.

1. Spiritual corruption happens when we allow ourselves to fall into a spiritual state of dull lethargy. "Since they see nothing serious to reproach themselves with, they fail to realize that their spiritual life has gradually turned lukewarm."

2. Another form of spiritual corruption is "a comfortable and self-satisfied form of blindness. Everything then appears acceptable: deception, slander, egotism and other subtle forms of self-centeredness, for 'even Satan disguises himself as an angel of light' (*2 Cor* 11:14)." This form of spiritual corruption "baptizes" things that lead people away from God. Have you ever seen this? Ever been afraid of it in you?

DISCERNMENT

SUMMARY: Discernment is the antidote Pope Francis offers against spiritual corruption. It is both a gift of the Holy Spirit and a spiritual practice. The Holy Father goes on in some length to describe different aspects of discernment.

An urgent need

1. Discernment is the ability to discern what is from God and what is from the devil. In today's world, which offers new options and possibilities at the most rapid pace in human history, discernment is essential. How do you tell the difference?

2. The Pope cautions that the devil often tempts us not to change when change is necessary, to leave things as they are, to opt for a rigid resistance to change. Can you remember experiencing that temptation?

Always in the light of the Lord

SUMMARY: Discernment is not reserved for monumental moments in life; it is needed even for the ordinary responsibilities and commitment of the day. To this end, the Pope recommends a daily examination of conscience.

1. The Pope recommends a daily examination of conscience, not just for each day's responsibilities and commitments, or sins committed, but also our striving for all that is great, better, and more beautiful. What would your examination of conscience include?

A supernatural gift

SUMMARY: Discernment has a wide reach and cannot be restricted to the insights of contemporary science or even the norms of the Church. A true discernment is an occasion of grace, a glimpse into "the meaning of my life before the Father." This can only be found with prolonged prayer.

1. True discernment is a deep prayer beyond even the sound norms of the Church. It "has to do with the meaning of my life before the Father who knows and loves me, with the real purpose of my life, that nobody knows better than he." Have you experienced or come close to this deep understanding?

Speak, Lord

SUMMARY: Discernment is a prayer in which we prepare ourselves to listen to the Lord speak to us. These are often words of challenge and change, that liberate us from the solutions of the past in service of the newness of the Gospel.

1. The Pope turns again to the Holy Spirit as the agent of discernment, speaking through prayer, our own hearts, the hearts and lives of others, even the realities of the world around us. We must remember that prayerful discernment must be born of a readiness to listen: to the Lord and to others, and to reality itself, which always challenges us in new ways. Listening to this Spirit requires great trust. To trust God this much we must know what frightens us, so what frightens you about trusting God?

The logic of the gift and of the cross

SUMMARY: Through the process of discernment, we learn how to accomplish our baptismal mission, so we ought not be surprised if it leads us in the footsteps of the Master, to the cross. In the mystery of the cross, of God's unconditional love, we attain holiness.

1. People engage in deep soul searching to discover how they can get more out of life. Christians engage in discernment, so they can recognize how they can accomplish the mission entrusted to them at their baptism. How do you describe the mission entrusted to you?

2. Pope Francis has a strong devotion to Mary, the Mother of Jesus. What do you know about Mary?

3. Pope Francis that to be a saint is to "share a happiness that the world will not take from us." Do you long to be a saint?

ABOUT THE AUTHORS

Pope Francis, Jorge Mario Bergolio, was born in Buenos Aires on December 17, 1936. On March 13, 2013, he became the bishop of Rome and the 266th pope of the Catholic Church.

Massimo Faggioli is full professor in the Department of Theology and Religious Studies at Villanova University (Philadelphia) and contributing editor to *Commonweal* magazine.

Catherine E. Clifford is professor of systematic and historical theology in the Faculty of Theology, Saint Paul University, Ottawa.

Mark-David Janus, CSP, PhD, is president and publisher of Paulist Press.